Psychoneuroplasticity Protocols
for Addictions

Psychoneuroplasticity Protocols for Addictions

A Clinical Companion for The Big Book

Frank Lawlis, PhD, A.B.P.P.
with Laura Martinez, LCDC-I, B.S

ROWMAN & LITTLEFIELD
Lanham • Boulder • New York • London

Published by Rowman & Littlefield
A wholly owned subsidiary of The Rowman & Littlefield Publishing Group, Inc.
4501 Forbes Boulevard, Suite 200, Lanham, Maryland 20706
www.rowman.com

Unit A, Whitacre Mews, 26-34 Stannary Street, London SE11 4AB

British Library Cataloguing in Publication Information Available

Library of Congress Cataloging-in-Publication Data

Lawlis, G. Frank, author
Psychoneuroplasticity protocols for addictions : a clinical companion for the big book / Frank Lawlis;
with Laura Martinez.
p. ; cm.
Companion volume to: Alcoholics Anonymous big book.
Includes bibliographical references and index.
ISBN 978-1-4422-4197-8 (cloth : alk. paper) -- ISBN 978-1-4422-4199-2 (ebook)
I. Martinez, Laura, 1986- , author. II. Alcoholics Anonymous big book. Complemented by (work):
III. Title. [DNLM: 1. Psychotherapy--methods. 2. Substance-Related Disorders--therapy. 3. Anxiety
Disorders--therapy. 4. Neuronal Plasticity. WM 270]
RC480.5
616.89'14--dc23
2014046210

Printed in the United States of America

Contents

List of Figures

Foreword

There has been much criticism leveled at the field of addiction treatment in recent years. With remarkable advances in neuroscience, medical technology, genomics, social science statistics, and pharmacology, we now know more about addictive illness and its treatment than at any other time in history. Yet these advances are not translating into improved clinical protocols for the addiction treatment workforce, and most importantly, are not resulting in improved outcomes for individuals seeking treatment for their addictive illness. There exists a marked disconnect in the "service-to-science" pathways stretching between the brilliant, ground-breaking research occurring around the globe and the dedicated, difficult work happening with addicts and alcoholics on the ground. This disconnect is apparent to anyone who takes more than a momentary look at the addiction treatment field, though it is not easy to remedy. The stigma attached to addiction (which still exists in very powerful ways) has left a lasting legacy on the creation, maturation, and consideration of addiction science and treatment. Moral questions, the erroneous notion that addiction is a choice, and the devastation left in the wake of the addict's/alcoholic's life sometimes make it hard for society to allocate the resources necessary to advance the field in the same ways that cancer, heart disease, diabetes, and even other mental health problems have advanced.

As a result of this stigma, the addiction treatment has long existed outside the general healthcare system. It has not been subject to the standards, norms, or oversight associated with what we understand as healthcare in America. Research on addiction and what works in its treatment have been vastly underfunded when one considers the public health cost that addiction exacts on society annually. There are few federal guidelines for the treatment of addiction and the licensure standards of addiction practitioners vary according to state. Until recently, what was known about treatment for addiction was largely anecdotal pseudo–science that was widely disregarded by anyone outside of the treatment industry. Instead of basing treatment recommendations on evidence-based practice, the field relied almost solely on the institutional wisdom of early treatment pioneers. This resulted in a stagnant, one-size-fits-all treatment model that often threw the "kitchen-sink" at those seeking help hoping that something would stick. Complicating this issue were competing definitions of addiction across the fields of medicine, psychology, sociology, and spirituality. What was known about addiction could be summed up in the following sentences. Spiritual transformation was happening in the rooms of Alcoholics Anonymous and other 12-Step fellowships leading to full remission and recovery from addictive illness. Some people entered a period of heavy use only to "age-out" of it. Medicating underlying disorders sometimes eased the intensity of drinking/use in an individual or ended it all together.

Lacking in these explanations of recovery, were the imperative questions of "how" and "why." It was not until the advent of modern neuroscience that the field of addiction had any answers. The past 20 years (beginning with George H. W. Bush's "Decade of the Brain" initiative in 1990) has seen the field of addiction research transformed. Increased funding to brain research and the leadership of the National Institute on Drug Abuse has finally moved addiction research to a platform from which to enact real change. We now understand that addiction is a disease of the brain, rooted in the complex interactions of neurotransmitters that are highly susceptible to interference of drugs of abuse. We understand that brain structure varies from person to person, making some individuals more prone to addictive illness. And most importantly, we know that the brain has a unique quality, its plasticity or ability to change. Finally, many of the questions about "how" and "why" a person becomes an addict or alcoholic are in reach of modern science.

However, we cannot stop there. Research that explains the occurrence of a disease does not always prescribe its treatment. And the distance between these poles is perhaps no greater in any other field of healthcare than it is in addiction treatment. While the stigma-fighting explanation of addiction as a brain disease and the potential to screen individuals according to neuro-anatomical structure is a huge contribution, the hope of many who suffer from addictive illness hangs on to one thing, the plasticity of the brain. But how do we change the brain, how do we tap into neuroplasticity to benefit the millions of Americans who are desperately trying to recover from the nightmare of addictive disease? How does this research move into practice?

Psychoneuroplasticity Protocols for Addiction is an answer to those questions. It is a book on the edge—a book that represents a tipping point in the translation of addiction science into practical, real-world applications for practitioners. It is a book that directly addresses service-to-science problems that the field of addiction treatment has struggled with for the past decade. It is a book that translates brain research into patient deliverables by explaining how to use the brain to fight addiction and improve recovery outcomes. And it does so while embracing the long-standing recovery culture that has been the only source of hope for addicts and alcoholics in the past fifty years.

There is not a more exciting time to work in the field of addiction science and addiction treatment than now. We are finally on the cusp of breakthroughs that are making a difference in the lives of those who are addicted, in the lives of their families, and on the vast socio-economic drains that this public health problem is wrecking on society. I have had the privilege to work alongside the authors of *Psychoneuroplasticity Protocols for Addiction* and have found myself re-energized by witnessing the changes in patient care, staff training, and outcomes that have accompanied their pilot work at a treatment center. This book, on the surface, outlines basic steps that can be implemented in any treatment service arena in the country without costly technology or intensive workforce investment. Digging deeper, however, this book is about something much more profound. It is about hope—hope that the work of two decades of brain science will finally reach those who need it most, hope that we finally have a tool that will give us a true advantage in the war on addiction, hope that lives lost to this disease every year will someday be stymied, and hope that *Psychoneuroplasticity Protocols in Addiction* is the first of many texts that stand on a tipping point pushing harder and harder toward that "paradigm shift" so badly needed in the field of addiction science and practice.

Amanda "Mandy" K. Baker, MS, LCDC
Vice-President for Clinical Services, Origins Recovery Center

Preface

In the last 30 years there has developed technology, such as EEG, S.P.E.C.T., and MRI imagery scans and computer capability, to the edge of the neurological edge. Up until now we have had only observations of behaviors and autopsies of cadavers on which to base our judgments of how the brain operates. Brain maps can now show us the magic of how it functions. We are on the cusp of knowing ourselves on the most complex biological levels and how we can make more of a difference in suffering.

This book is not meant to fill in the blanks about what we know about the brain in scientific terms, however. This book is about the therapeutic applications as we observe constructive or destructive results. For example, the effects of pressured oxygen on improved cognitive functions or the long results from electric shock therapy on prolonged cognitive memory problems. Oddly enough, the techniques we have discovered are not particularly new in technology but the understandings are new. It is possible and probable that what our ancestors discovered centuries earlier has a scientific base. They practiced from an empirical base of success, not so much from a theoretical perspective. From the drum beats of ancient rituals to the mantras and shamanistic journeys, we are struck with the intuitive language that exists between nature and the brain that emerges from new experience. The art of healing was taught long before the scientific age.

As the healing community nears the stage of "evidence-based" therapies we enter a precarious edge of uncertain expectations as far as what research models will convince us about what works and what doesn't. It is certain that ethics often runs counter to trying to prove some things with human beings. For example, one of the gold standards we use in medicine is the randomized control vs. experimental group analysis. You give one group a pill that is supposed to get rid of tumors and another group a placebo for comparison.

Most of our medical tools cannot be used in this way because you can't treat people the same way you treat rats or seed (note: these models of research were derived from agricultural literature). For example, you can't treat stem cells replacement for cancer patients with placebos. It is well known that placebos do have an effect in the belief of the patients. It seems unethical to not offer the best remedies you have for patients, especially if they are paying for treatment and coming for the best they can get.

There are great debates over these methods and one that is highly contested is the univariate versus the multivariate approach. The univariate is the approach of testing one variable at a time; the multivariate method is testing a lot of variables at one time and seeing how they correlate in function. Both are valuable but testing one variable at a time takes a very long time, especially if you are doing brain research. A good example is this basic question: how does the brain work to make an organism behave? If you take the fruit fly (*Drosophila melanogaster* species), which has about 10,000 neurons, and try to analyze which of these neurons cause behavior, the human eye and brain simply cannot see that many connections at once. But if you apply a multivariate technique (principle components) there would be approximately twenty-nine combinations that correlate to simple acts of rolling and turning behavior. Human behavior and brain neuron analysis are far from applying this technique, since we have over 200 billion neurons and obviously more complex behaviors.

Our ignorance of what technology has yet to provide and what human wisdom has yet to reveal perhaps remains our greatest obstacle. The United States believes in technology as our best bet in the healing science to the tune of spending twice as much as the second highest nation (Japan) for medical cures yet the United States rarely ranks in the top ten countries for overall medical health by the World Health Organization. More often than not we usually don't get higher than twentieth.

The economic issues loom heavily in these matters as insurance carriers and individuals search for the best efficient treatment. Again, the knotty problems of human beings persist because many physical problems and diseases are curable within a specified timeframe. If you break your arm, there are remedies that will help the body cure itself within weeks. But the categories of diseases that are chronic pose another issue economically. Addiction belongs in this frame because the recovery is a lifetime process with complications of underlying psychological and biological complexities that have a healing process of their own.

It remains our quest to make our society safer from disastrous consequences of disease and destructive life styles. We must keep an open mind to any thought or event that leads us to another great discovery. We must have courage to struggle for truth.

In spite of the new technology that has recently brought us so many advances; the primary components to transformation into healthier states still remain as love and hope. The role of science has given us a broader scope of reasoning and allowed us to have deeper appreciation of the wonders of the brain and mind.

This book was written as a manual for professionals and para-professionals to learn the application of psychoneuroplasticity (PNP) principles for their suffering patients. It is a science-based therapy but the heart of what makes it work is similar to all other therapies, including everything from surgery to internal medicine. That is the compassion and empathy a therapist portrays to the patient.

It is the hope of therapists to practice with the spirit of service to the mind and body, not with the attitude of "proving something." It should be remembered that the body is designed to heal itself, given the right support. We can help it find its way, but we must respect what we can and what we can't help. We can serve as a channel by using the tools of nurturing the internal core of the miracle of life and recovery.

There are a hundred thoughts on each page of this book that can be used as tools for either the therapist and/or the healer. For some, the discoveries can be immediate, but for others, the process might require some scientific fact or experience that connects the dots. This book offers many avenues for us all.

Acknowledgments

The authors wish to acknowledge their roles as scribes in the collaborative work of Dr. Barbara Peavey in her pioneering clinical applications and defining the architecture of psychoneuroplasticity (PNP). She is a great teacher to us all as we strive to create new roads over the barriers to recovery of addiction. Without her leadership and contributions this book would have not been written. We also want to thank the wonderful support of Ben Levenson who is a visionary of PNP applications in the recovery setting whose heart is always directed for the patients' welfare. Advice and support given by wordsmith Anthony Haskins has been a great help in moving this book from start to finish. A warm thank you goes out to Josh Slay for his vast knowledge and experience with the Twelve Steps, which has been incorporated in the text.

Disclaimer

The case examples in this book have been taken from composite case studies and the names have been used from a randomized method. Any resemblance of any name or case description to any person is only by coincidence and does not relate to any real person, living or dead. The author and publisher specifically disclaim all responsibility for any liability, loss, or risk, personal or otherwise, which is incurred as a consequence, directly or indirectly, of the use and application of any of the contents of this book.

Part I

The Brain and Addiction

The brain is the last of the frontiers. With its 200 billion neurons it makes up our individual intellects, personalities, cognitive functions, motor activities, and dreams. It is far more complicated than space and much more mysterious. Even an ant has a brain that is more complex than the most complex computer.

While it is wondrous, the brain can also be misaligned from the pure predictions of our projected lives. That is one difference we, as humans, possess and do so as a natural developmental step in our lives. Other animals stay within their consciousness and boundaries of their nature. A dog doesn't fly an airplane, a cat does not invent new diets, and a horse does not decide to live in a house. Animals live within their nature, but the brains of humans are unique and not always healthy.

The exciting events of the past ten years has been the developments of methodology for changing our brains to be healthier and smarter, to make better choices, and to escape the tragedies of early mistakes and minimize fears. This can be the era of breakthroughs to deliver our true potentials and turn the wheel from generational abuse to renewal.

ONE

The Psychoneuroplasticity Concept Introduction in Addiction

In the United States approximately 23.2 million souls, which accounts for 8.3 percent of the population over the age of twelve, are using some form of addictive substance of drugs or alcohol (Volkow 2009) which may not be particularly surprising. An estimated 76.4 million people worldwide meet the criteria for alcohol use disorders (AUDs) (World Health Organization [WHO] 2004), and 15.3 million meet the criteria for drug use disorders (Loftis and Huckans 2013). Besides addiction disorders, substance abuse and dependence are linked to a variety of medical disorders, including increased prevalence of infectious diseases, (Kresina et al. 2005) hepatitis C viral infections (Klevens et al. 2012), and cancer, heart, and liver diseases.

However, what is more alarming is the rate of citizens becoming dependent on medically prescribed medications at an epidemic rate. The deaths related to prescription drugs now outnumber the deaths associated with cocaine and heroin combined in twenty-nine states and Washington, D.C. The consequences of this misuse and abuse cost the nation 53.4 billion dollars in terms of lost productivity, medical costs, and criminal justice processing (Prescription Drug Abuse). This problem will become more complex as more states are legalizing marijuana as well as other medical drugs for mental stress.

These data describe the single impact of individuals with this terrible disease, but the real tragedy goes beyond the single case. Virtually every family member is affected negatively by one substance-abusing person. A parent can permanently injure their children or a spouse psychologically with the constant insecurity and undermining of self-regard, crippling all those involved. There is a clinical variable related to being a "child of a drug addict or alcoholic" highly related to life-long impact. Moreover, the influence of abuse and addiction within a family unit can carry on into future generations, either genetically or psychologically. It has been a problem in the past, and it is guaranteed to continue creating major problems for the future. But unlike other disease categories, this is not an issue that can be resolved with a magic pill or serum.

There is a rampant increase in cases of pregnant women addicted to pain medications (Kaltenbach, Berghella, and Finnegan 1998) which has led to the creation of medical services for the babies born with an addiction to these drugs. It is not difficult to guess what the outcomes are when these babies reach their own liberties to addictions. The addiction cycle goes on.

This is a problem that destroys families and the happiness in their lives in every class of our society along with the rest of the world. There has not been an advance in the treatment of addiction since before World War II. Not only are all of us supporting the devastation with our tax dollars, but we are also confusing the issues of the individual's choice to get "high" and the responsibilities of consequences.

To be sure, much of the problems in finding solutions can be found by our understanding between the cause of addiction and the disease status of addiction. Many diseases can be discussed as having lifestyle causes, such as smoking and cancer, overeating and obesity, stressful living and heart disease, and so on. There is a difference between "using drugs" and the term "addiction disease." Society has been frustrated by attempting to control addiction by legal means, such as the prohibition laws of the 1920s and the "War on Drugs."

It appears that people have a desire to transcend their ordinary state of conscious reality at times, and one of the ways is related to using drugs of some kind. Music and spiritual rituals are the two most historical, but are a lot less efficient than smoking, taking a drink, or taking a pill. Addiction has been in human history since Biblical times, and has led to the downfalls of many civilizations. The only dent that has been seen in the abuse of substances has not been legal but educational. It would be advantageous to consider addiction as a chronic disease rather than an acute disease because of the long-term development to find resolution rather than a short-term remedy.

Regardless of the critical factors of personal lifestyles and rich development of values, the primary purposes of this book is that unless some new human function appears so that this human need to attempt to escape pain and fear disappears, drug substances and alcohol will be used in our future to mask or numb life away.

The next question is how to distinguish those people who will or will not become a victim to the substance abuse stage and eventually into a disease state. Humans change our complete physiological systems every seven years and likely change their psychological status more often than that, depending on our securities in our work, marriage, and age-related interests. There is no present "prevention" step for addiction that can be articulated with any sense of success.

This book is about treating addiction as defined as a disease and there are very exciting chapters. The challenges for treatment can be understood and resolved into the recovery state and it has worked many times.

DEFINING ADDICTION, THE DISEASE

The most ancient definition of addiction has been seen as a spiritual problem, such as possession of the devil, soul degeneration, and so on. This explanation is continued in many parts of the world, yet has failed to explain the mystery of recovery. Some later thinking considers addiction to be psychological collapse, but this did not explain the ability of the person to appear to function episodically. There was some interest in finding a virus but none has been found.

There are inconsistent and opposing definitions of the addiction disease, which might explain the inconsistency among the treatments. Nevertheless, all have some validity. It is important that one recognizes the efforts to understand the disease state of addiction from the many healing professions' perspectives.

(1) *Diagnostic and Statistical Manual (DSM) of Mental Disorders Criteria* (American Psychiatric Association 2000): Substance dependence is when an individual persists in use of alcohol or other drugs despite problems related to use of the substance; then the substance dependence may be diagnosed. Compulsive and repetitive use may result in tolerance to the effect of the drug and withdrawal symptoms when use is reduced or stopped. Along with substance abuse, this is considered a Substance Use Disorder. A maladaptive pattern of substance use leading to clinically significant impairment or distress, as manifested by one (or more) of the following, occurring within a 12 month period:

1. Recurrent substance use resulting in failure to fulfill major role obligations at work, school, or home.
2. Recurrent substance use in situations in which it is physically hazardous.
3. Recurrent substance related legal problems.
4. Continued substance use despite having persistent or recurrent social or interpersonal problems caused by the effects of the substance.

Seen from a psychiatric perspective, addiction is defined as functional behaviors in which the person has lost the ability to function adequately in various settings and deviates significantly from societal norms as a result of the behavior of consuming a drug or set of drugs. It would be fair to conclude that resolution of the problem would be an intervention to rehabilitate a person back to a state of normal function. The psychiatrist's remedies would likely include additional prescriptions to either diminish or facilitate the brain's abilities to enable successful performances to normality.

(2) *The Psychodynamic Model* (Khantzian 2003): This describes drug abusers as "self-medicating." Drug abuse is a symptom of underlying psychological problems and drug use is a maladaptive psychological coping strategy. Drug abusers need to resolve internal conflict, and when they do, drug use will be unnecessary.

According to this brief description of the Psychodynamic Model, the problem of addiction has little to do with the substance but the reason for using it to cope with premorbid problems, such as anxiety or depression. Although this model could appear to deny the toxic damage of drug abuse itself or of the neurological processing that engenders the logical processing, which might be genetic or part of the psychodynamics themselves, the model implies that psychotherapy will do away with the need for drugs and the addiction will resolve itself.

(3) *National Institute on Drug Abuse and Addiction* (National Institute on Drug Abuse 2000): Addiction is defined as a chronic relapsing brain disease that is characterized by compulsive drug seeking and use, despite harmful consequences. It is considered a brain disease because drugs change the brain—they change its structure and how it works. These brain changes can be long lasting, and can lead to the harmful behaviors seen in people who abuse drugs.

This may be considered the molecular model of addiction because it appears to focus on the neurological structure of addiction as a static condition. As recently as ten years ago the brain was considered to be at the end of its growth period by age eighteen and any change was an automatic subtraction of function. Like a computer, it operated the same from birth to death. While this model has a scientific basis, it does not serve for a rehabilitation model other than to change the brain itself without the goal of long term sobriety. There is little doubt of its validity, but it appears to leave out the human spirit, which is vital to recovery.

(4) *The Social Model of Addiction* (Niaura, R. 2000): Drug use is a learned behavior and people use drugs because it is modeled by others and perpetuated through peer pressure. Environmental effects lead to drug use (advertising, etc.). Drug use is a maladaptive relationship negotiation strategy.

While there is a basis for assuming that social rituals may include some drug or alcohol usage, it is also true that the majority of these rituals do not result in the disease of addiction. Even if the participants get drunk or lose the abilities to function (drive, cognitively calculate solutions, conduct effective negotiations, etc.) the disease of addiction would need to be more inclusive. However, it should be noted that it is often necessary to permanently separate family and friend enablers from those afflicted by addiction because of the damaging impact on motivation and self-control.

(5) *Medilexicon's Medical Dictionary* (Lippincott Williams and Wilkins 2006): "Addiction is habitual psychological or physiologic dependence on a substance or practice that is beyond voluntary control. Withdrawal has many meanings, one of which is a psychological and/or physical syndrome caused by the abrupt cessation of the use of a drug in a habituated person."

While addiction is often a mental obsession to substances, it is not usually on one substance, but on the state of mind one desires. Whatever substance or substances that are available that will accomplish that feat will be used. But the essential point of this definition is the lack of voluntary control in the mental obsession for a specific state of mind. In this sense, one can be a "dry drunk" and still obsess for a state that may go ungratified but still maintains power over a person.

(6) *Alcoholics Anonymous Twelve-Step Version* (Wilson 2013): Addiction is a threefold disease of the mind, body, and spirit. The body undergoes a physical allergy, in which the body has no control with the substance. The mind undergoes mental obsession in which the person has no choice. The spirit undergoes spiritual malady in which the person is restless, irritable, and discontent until the addict can use the substance again.

This definition of addiction has been chosen as the starting point to recovery. While the statement was made based on very old science, it remains to be true in its underlying process of resolution. By integrating the body, mind, and spirit in its description of the complex levels of change required, it defines the steps of transition needed for recovery. There is also the wisdom of experience that supports the concept of being a victim to the disease, which underlines the need for transformation and shifting to a higher level of support that can be met through a network of workers united for the same goals.

(7) *American Society of Addiction Medicine* (American Society of Addiction Medicine 1996): Addiction is a primary, chronic disease of brain reward, motivation, memory, and related circuitry. Dysfunction in these circuits leads to characteristic biological, psychological, social, and spiritual manifestations. This is reflected in an individual pathologically pursuing reward and/or relief by substance use and other behaviors. Addiction is characterized by inability to consistently abstain, impairment in behavioral control, diminished recognition of significant problems with one's behaviors and interpersonal relationships, and a dysfunctional emotional response. Like other chronic diseases, addiction often involves cycles of relapse and remission. Without treatment or engagement in recovery activities, addiction is progressive and can result in disability or premature death."

This definition serves as a basis for the "psychoneuroplasticity" model of this book by providing experiences that appear to have a direct impact on the neuro-complex relating to addiction. The association to addiction as a "brain disease" no longer has to be debated, but an action plan can be designed to influence the seat of logic and motivation; however, some healing must be placed during the recovery phase so that optimal functions of the neurological system can be utilized. For example, if the occipital lobe (where vision orientation is normally located) is damaged and one's vision is impaired, it may offer nothing but frustration to attempt vision training. A proper process has to be provided and integration of the three levels of body, mind, and spirit in an effective treatment plan.

THE PSYCHONEUROPLASTICITY DEFINITION

As repeated in explanation, all of these definitions have validities associated with the structure and concept of addiction, yet have not developed the consistency for success or the expectancy to meet the new demand noted in the introduction. The origins of the concept of psychoneuroplasticity (PNP) began with the observations in rehabilitation or physical medicine, a departmental category of medicine related to physical rehabilitation focus.

This field of training was so appealing because of the continuous astounding events that might be considered miracles if you believe in a non-redeemable injury world. In traumatic events, such as the sudden inability to talk because of a brain stroke or injury, one would expect that part of the brain that governed that function would be destroyed. However, the brain has backup functions so speech and other physical abilities can be employed by other parts of the brain. Moreover, through nerve cell generation, called neuronal genesis, new patterns can be formed to perform old and new functions. People with major damage can learn to walk again through these new avenues of nerve connection. Patients can learn new ways to remember old methods and information. These processes are known as neuroplasticity.

To expand this concept to a higher form of brain function, psychological performance, and cognitive performance, the same principles serve to generate new pathways for emotional and mental functions. People who have PTSD barriers to sobriety can correct the emotional trauma associated with the events so as to dissolve the stifling fears that hamper normal psychological states. The fog that clouds the judgment of people detoxing can be cleared and the healing of the brain can begin.

Just like emotional trauma can create damaged pathways in seconds or years, a process that might take years to resolve in order for a person to break through the mental obsession can be accomplished in a matter of years or minutes. The patterns that might have started the process toward addiction can be detoured so that old physiological and psychological processes can be virtually restructured toward healthy patterns.

Before this section is seen as a panacea, these techniques are not in themselves a program for addiction recovery. But they can be seen as methods to break through the underlying barriers of addiction recovery. Recovery requires transformation, such as in the Twelve Steps, but PNP can be a critical tool for the barriers of mental obsessions, fears, barriers of anxiety, resolutions of past psychological patterns, and the healing of the brain. Most important, these methods are well within the time frames of rehab programs, making them an integrated effort within the total efforts of a curriculum of medical, social, and other counseling techniques.

This book is to offer the underlying basis for PNP in the treatment of addiction and drug dependency. In the following chapters, these approaches will be discussed with the objective in application to eliminate the barriers people with addiction have on the journey toward recovery.

FORTHCOMING PNP METHODS

Transformation into Recovery

Recovery is a process of change that comes from the inside out as change of brain patterns occur. However, addiction is seldom a one-sided issue because of the sociological influences as well as the biological and psychological layers of a human being throughout life. A human's constructive change toward wholeness has always been a multiple level process and in concert with the desired result of the process that has been the basics stated in *The Big Book* (Alcoholics Anonymous 1976) from the awareness of being helpless by one's own ego and brain disease to new and healthy relationships. This is known as transformation.

Transformation takes many forms and all forms should be tolerated. Transformation is of great importance in the process. Although immediate change is hoped for and even observed to be genuine by the family and friends, the real work can be described much as the art of shamanism. In that metaphoric context, the individual has to die and be recreated in new form and purpose. The new form is not returned as "fixed" to the point earlier in life but better, healthier, and wiser. There are many examples to describe this process.

The Principles of Psychoneuroplasticity

In this chapter, the basic principles of PNP will be discussed with four simple principles of neuron plasticity. These principles apply to all stages of neuron development, including changing habits and emotional components in everyday life, and follow the same methods in rehabilitation medicine.

Defining the Neurological Pathways of Addiction

This chapter more closely defines the neurological pathways of addictions and how they are formed. These are based on clinical research as well as animal studies in which rats can be taught to be addicted to alcohol or drugs, but once addicted through brain patterns, they can be turned back to non-addicted behavior. Of course, rats are not people and environments cannot be controlled as in these studies, but these studies point very clearly to the understanding of PNP and addictions with humans. As a reminder to the reader that as excited as one can be about these developing sciences, PNP is a part of a total effort and is not intended to be the total answer to recovery; however, this is definitely a vital part of the whole picture.

Overcoming Anxiety Barriers

In a brief analysis of clients, it has been noted that anxiety and fear has been the most frequent barrier to recovery and relapse. This may be due to the mounting stress and tension that is associated with failures of the past. There are definite observations that most of our patients have not had any direction in managing their stress levels, other than by self-medicating with drugs. More important in our approaches, very few have had any models in which they could recognize any effort that might be successful rather than using substances harmful to their health. To some extent many of these patients have been labelled with "personality disorders" because of their resistance to emotionally develop because fear and anxiety overwhelmed them and/or they were culturally blocked to develop normally by their families and friends.

The topic of anxiety and fear requires some methods of dealing with traumatic events that block a person's life development, keeping them "stuck" or trapped in a time period. Better known as Post Traumatic Stress Disorder (PTSD), PNP methods can show immediate relief of disoriented stress and allows the patient to proceed with his or her life planning. The kinds of trauma can be anything from rape to child abuse or neglect to witnessing horrific scenes of family terror to losing a career to unjust purposes or the grief of losing a significant person through death or unfortunate circumstances.

Stress can be a normal obstacle in life and few of us escape it. Facing fear with appropriate tools can make us stronger, but without a hint of resistance, it can beat us down and kill us literally. Sometimes addiction is the only way of survival for a short period of time. Certainly anxiety and fear can serve as critical barriers to transformation.

Depressive Barriers to Transformation

Sometimes depression can be related to a genetic or organic feature in one's personality in which part of the brain has "low voltage" in the joy regions. This is another way of describing a "sad brain." This would be a neurological landmine for addiction because of the high need for stimulation and the potential fixation on drugs and alcohol for stimulating what might be considered normal for the individual. There has been evidence that this does occur at times, and one of the most exciting results of PNP. Using sound as another stimulus for these areas of the brain, the person can feel joy and happiness through these same patterns as drugs but without toxicity or the devastating consequences of use. It has become possible to actually train the brain to be happy.

Another source of depression, especially among women, is persistent low self-esteem created by social neglect, abuse, bad nutrition, or just bad luck of being raised in a poorly supported environment. Perhaps the most potentially damaging, however, is the internal distorted mind that twists reality such that all events are perceived as negative aspects of self. Cognitive psychology, mantras, and even strong aromas can be used as PNP to change these neurological patterns and begin to change the underlying self-image dimensions to positive ones.

One neurological feature of depression that can be understood is the mental trap of rumination, the obsession pattern in which thoughts are magnified in a cycle of repeated thoughts, usually manifesting negative ideas. These OCD patterns are usually associated with anxiety; however, the results of loss of production and never-ending loss of control over one's mind eventually whittles away at self-control until one gives up. This is a repetitive barrier to transformation.

The Adolescent Brain Barrier

It is not unusual to see teenagers who fall into the arena of addiction in the path of stifled development. It is also not unusual to see adults in their forties with the same immaturity of a teenager who lives the life of high stimulation and runs on the need to find the next thrill. This is what is related to what might be called the "Peter Pan" syndrome in which the person doesn't want to grow up. Drugs often are associated with this dynamic, such as marijuana. These individuals are certainly challenges to the recovery system that demands they grow up emotionally with basic motivations toward sound goals.

Multi-polar and Rage Barriers

These brain patterns are described as cyclical behavioral patterns that are similar to the euphoria/depression bipolar description; however, the cycles usually relate to rages. This neurological pattern has been related to levels of toxicity in the brain, and would be easily understood through the toxicities of drugs and alcohol. PNP methods include nutrition and supplements for lowering toxicity of the brain as well as possible treatments.

Spiritual Barriers

Defined as one's sense of mission of something greater than oneself and being loved or acknowledged as a special person as one's spirituality, it would be obvious that the courage and staying responsible for sobriety would need to be based on highest levels in motivation. It is one of the first steps in the Twelve Steps sequence for an acceptance of a possible higher power. Being the basis for transformation, the barriers to spiritual acceptance usually relate to an early separation from a sense of love and safety, then distorted to guilt, shame, and suppression of hope.

Although there have been claims for a region of the brain regarded as the spiritual components, spirituality comes from escape from the ego demands of addiction and learning to love again. Many conversions to the higher power of the client's understanding have been able to be identified individually once the barriers are released and a safe place is found internally. These processes can be accomplished through imagery and finding one's internal compass.

SUMMARY

Seen in earlier times as a psychological or spiritual disorder, with the use of brain maps it has been discovered that there are stages of healing, and the first stage is the healing of the brain. Consistently, addiction damages the brain directly and from inflammation indirectly. In addition, the discovery of some brain precursors to addiction has been identified, such as low-functioning pleasure centers and overly sensitive pain receptor sites that have a high correlation to addictive behaviors. Hence, the introductions of psychoneuroplasticity methods have been applied. The basic concept is the alteration of brain patterns that can be directly constructive in healing of brain tissue as well as modifying behavioral patterns. Instead of trying to cure problems from addictive pills to be solved with even more pills, the destructive patterns can be changed and directed with such stimulations as sound frequencies, meditation models, neurofeedback, positive cognitive shifts, and many other exercises. Most of these methods can be performed by counselors and therapists who work in the health care system today. There is overwhelming evidence that these models work alongside the AA Twelve Step Program, thus augmenting existing beliefs of transformation by eliminating barriers to success.

This book can be used to understand the brain and addiction, but the protocols within can be applied to make transformative differences in people's lives. Like all therapies, one approach may work better for one person than for another person. Consistently these therapies are to be shared through love and compassion.

TWO

Transformation

Spiritual Awakening

Fredrick grew up as your typical all-American teenager whose dreams and aspirations were inspired by his dad's successes as a businessman. He loved and admired his father greatly and hoped to be a small business administrator starting out and imagined a future partnership with his dad in an enterprising company. He went on to college where he majored in business administration and equipped himself with a very high grade-point average. He was ambitious to say the least and in his four years of college he earned his bachelor's and master's degree on a fast track curriculum.

In spite of Fredrick's best efforts in his studies, his father died in his junior year of college after a yearlong bout with pancreatic cancer and was to never see him graduate. By the steady support of his fraternity brothers and the love of his wife-to-be, he was able to reach his educational goal despite this hardship. Although the dream of a having a future partnership with his father was gone, it was not forgotten. To make his struggle for his goal even more confusing, Frederick found out that his father died in bankruptcy, which undermined his tremendous respect for his father as a businessman and began to cause him to doubt his own abilities to attain his goals.

Because of his superior education advantage over his competitors and his amazing organizational abilities, along with some very good luck, he rose fast in the career ladder and by his second year he had the title of "Director of Research and Development." He quickly learned the habits of executive behavior, such as consulting with political contacts of major influence, writing ambitious grants and proposals, and consuming large amounts of alcohol at business parties. He was the big man in his field at a young age and enjoyed the spoils of expense accounts, power, and prestige. His state of affairs was a double-plus feature of his status and ego.

For the next two years it seemed he could do no wrong, but then began a series of events that were to spiral out of control and eventually to his demise. He used his new found power to defeat his own boss, one of his greatest early-on supporters, and worse, he began to cut ties with his friends, becoming increasingly insensitive to others and thus unknowingly became his own worst enemy. He made salary bonuses subject to his own subjective needs rather than nurturing mutual cooperation. In essence, Fredrick lost himself in his new self-concept as an executive whose power was absolute. In spite of all of his energies and good ideas, he made a tragic misuse of his power with a younger intern which led to him being demoted in a major way. To Fredrick, it was the end of his career, and his self-image as he defined it. Needless to say, he was devastated both financially and interpersonally.

After some time working as a typical "underling," as he called it, he decided to find another job where he could have a fresh start. He was successful in finding a new position on his first try by contacting an accomplished frat brother who knew his potential and was willing to start him out at a reduced salary, more in line with Frederick's experience and early career stage. He left his suite of offices and affairs to move to another part of the country, but the transition was not easy. He pursued various proposals and grants out of desperation for pride more than the mission, all of which were denied. His future was dimming fast and he could only see himself as a failure, perhaps even worse off than his father.

It was at this time that he began drinking anything that burned the emotions out of what he was experiencing. Whatever was strongest was his drink of the day. Gin, vodka, whiskey, rum, or red wine were his usual choices and he began drinking as soon as his workday ended. Each day he was in a whirlwind of emotions and each passing moment he was in a fog. Needless to say, he was not the potential star of the coming year. His faithful wife would soon leave him for a more stable future as his drinking took priority over his family life. His alcohol had become his mistress as he then began to secretively drink during work hours more and more which eventually led to him losing his job and giving up custody of his three children who were deprioritized to the point of abuse. He was an embarrassment to himself; drowning in his despair he had alcohol as his only coping mechanism.

Though he had no friends or family around, he was not alone. The never-ceasing voices in his head reminded him of his bashed dreams and failures as a father, husband, friend, businessman, and productive citizen. Being young and a drunk was worse than being old because he didn't have the excuse of bad breaks over a long period of time, rather, he had been the cause of his own demise. His spirit was broken and he was lost in a maze of confusion where alcohol was his only numbing escape.

Frederick was smart enough to know that he needed help, but he was convinced that *his* drinking did not add up to what he defined as an addiction. He was beginning to realize that his drinking would never give him anything other than serious grief and more problems, so when he saw a homeless vagrant chugging whiskey on the street corner while on his way to the liquor store, his life flashed before his eyes and realized that was his future if he continued this way. In that moment, he turned around, went home and decided to muster the discipline to sober up. He stopped cold turkey and started attending A.A. meetings where he got honest with himself and others telling his story of how he started his life with too much success and not enough humility. He started to feel painful emotions again and went through the behavior of a dry drunk, feeling worse every day. That old familiar voice still called to him from the back of his mind with messages of the delicious taste of being numb to his depression and how just a few drinks wouldn't do any harm.

Frederick was neither stupid nor crazy so he was fully aware of the consequences of another drink, yet on the anniversary date of his divorce, he relapsed. The precipitating event was not traumatic, just him home alone after a visitation with the kids and nothing left to do in the evening welcomed the regret and depression of a failed life. Just one drink and his body went into automatic pilot as he relished the state of mind where he could extinguish all mental pain and be "himself" again. Four weeks later he was in a detox program starting over with new promises and the certainty that he could not drink one drink or he would re-enter the slippery slope of addiction once again.

Frederick's story is not a new one and probably identical to thousands of people whose addictions have become the master of their lives, drunk or sober. The addictive substance has reprogrammed their brains to be constant monitors of their lifestyles so that they can avoid temptations, especially situations where they can seek refuge from their stressors. Unfortunately, there are many people whose brains are susceptible to addictive lives, and they cannot adopt the "walking the edge" lifestyle because of their substance abuse propensities. The result of adopting this perspective is not an optimistic mindset. What often happens is that they have to make a decision out of desperation in their lives to take action and seek help to live or to die from substance abuse or live the worse of alternatives, to live half a life.

TRANSFORMATION

To live the temporary gratification life where addiction controls you is without question a destructive path. The alternative is to go through a total life transformation of one's self and one's values so that pain relief ceases to be the only motive. To transform is to convert your brain, body, and spirit into a new state. According to the American Heritage Dictionary of the English language (Mifflin 2000) definition, transformation is the marked change of a person in character, values, and physical aspects. The mathematical definition is a great metaphor, which states that transformation is the replacement of variables in an algebraic expression by their values in terms of another set of variables.

In addiction medicine, "transformation" can be interchanged with a "transformative change" and the "protocol" is the steps or rituals that lead to transformation or the processes to go through in order to stabilize change in one's life. The decision may be made by numerous avenues; however, the decision sets the person's single focus in life on the path to conversion of motivations and attitudes. This transformation may or may not be vulnerable to relapse per se, but it involves the urgency to change one's life dramatically. The catalyst for the transformation could be a vision, such as the Burning Bush through which God allegedly spoke to Moses to send him off to serve as a leader and guide to free the slaves (New International Version, Exodus 2–4. 2012). It could be a dream or a guide who leads you to perform curative acts, such as Dr. Phil and his "wake-up" calls to rebuild his guests' lives. The transpersonal "moment" may be a disease which serves as a catalyst for change to be defined psychologically through different thinking and perceptual patterns. Physiological changes have been reported as evidence along with feedback that corrective behavior has been done, such as cancer tumors diminishing, a heart repairing itself, and nerve regeneration.

There is consciousness in every fiber of our bodies and this is not just contained within our bodies, but also within everything that surrounds us. This consciousness can communicate to us through visions, dreams, other people or even such things as a "coincidence" that strikes you as interesting. It could also communicate through a medical professional that takes the time to listen, care, and provide an action plan toward health. Perhaps this is the essence or source of what is called the "transpersonal moment" which opens the gateway for transformation.

In addiction disease states, there appears to be a critical moment in which a person makes the decision to change, making available resources within and external to themselves. It makes sense that the chronicity of addiction is enabled through a life choice and habits, making a shift in the disease to be dependent on a shift in these factors. The decision itself is of enormous transpersonal medicine interest because of its manifest changes in a disease. In alcoholism, this is often referred to as "hitting rock bottom." Conscious decision making and the motivation to maintain the vigil of habit change may not account for all the variance in recovery, but it is certainly a necessary factor in all rehabilitation outcomes.

ANTECEDENT ACTIONS THAT BRING
TRANSFORMATIVE MOMENTS

The antecedent conditions that lead to these life-changing moments are categorized below, although many have co-conspiring factors:

Prophet of Things to Come if Life Style Does Not Change

As seen in movies or read in Charles Dickens's *A Christmas Carol* (2009), the Spirit of Christmas Future frightens Scrooge into changing the way he hoards his riches and transforming him into a generous man capable of receiving and giving love. It is often a psychological strategy to give a future negative image to a person whose lifestyle is extremely unconstructive in order for them to see the damage they may do in their life and to others.

There are many patients with addictions who illustrate this "moment," usually in the second half of their lives when they wake up to the reality that getting drunk or high when they are dealing with conflict may numb themselves out to the anxiety or frustrations but it will not resolve the issues in their lives and usually creates even more problems. In fact, this reaction will only delay their happiness and life progress longer and the costs mount quickly. They begin to understand the need to "grow up" and face themselves and their responsibilities.

The experience was evident in working with Lorna who was a heavy drinker and used alcohol to deal with the many stressors in her life such as a bad marriage and a frustrating dead-end job. After many years of constant alcohol abuse, she discovered her kidneys were shutting down. Alcohol was now her worst enemy and was seriously threatening her survival. Being a resourceful person, she immediately stopped bar hopping and buying alcohol at the store, but in her case it was not the craving but rather the loneliness that was her major challenge since her only friends were her drinking buddies who still maintained their alcoholic lifestyles.

After treatment, Lorna gave up both her alcohol crutch as well as her friendships and replaced them with more productive skills such as exercise, breathing, and meditation. She has been free of her addiction for over ten years now and is healthy in all respects, including finding true happiness in a remarkable new life mission of compassion for others.

Potential Mission of Life as Seen from a Higher Source

Teachers, coaches, and counselors can be amazing agents of transpersonal transformation. Many times young adults have dropped out of education and life because they felt they were unable to reach the goals set up for them by their parents, or even themselves. Tom illustrates this issue very well. He had dropped out of his freshman year of college when he started failing his courses and later stopped going altogether. It doesn't take a psychologist to guess what else he was doing, though there was some indication that his involvement was more in denial of his failures than merely to get high, and that was proven to be the case.

Given some tutoring and counseling to teach him how to learn more efficiently as well as a lot of powerful support, he got traction the following year by making some changes in his life direction and his majors (from pre-law to pre-veterinary) and graduated as expected, with a strong sense of pride and appreciation.

A better known story not related to addiction but with the same point is found in John 5:1-8. (Bible, H. 1984) Jesus went up to Jerusalem for a feast of the Jews. There in Jerusalem near the Sheep Gate was a pool, which in Aramaic is called Bethesda and which is surrounded by five covered colonnades. Here a great number of disabled people used to lay—the blind, the lame, and the paralyzed. One who was there had been an invalid for thirty-eight years. When Jesus saw him lying there and learned that he had been in this condition for a long time, he asked him, "Do you want to get well?" "Sir," the invalid replied, "I have no one to help me into the pool when the water is stirred. While I am trying to get in, someone else goes down ahead of me." Then Jesus said to him, "Get up! Pick up your mat and walk." At once the man was cured; he picked up his mat and walked.

Awakening of the Spirit Within

For centuries cultures have been designing rituals around the concept of discovering the inner healing guide that resides deep within ourselves and is ready to act as an internal compass through our obstacles and struggles. It is usually masked by our egos (need for control) and fear (fear of being out of control); however, by implementing methods for subverting those forces (meditation, consciousness control, guided imagery, etc.) and thus making contact with that internal healing spirit is always positive and averts the need for drugs to achieve that level of consciousness. For many people suffering from alcoholism and addiction, the spiritual path has been the primary source of survival and possibly one of brain transformation, which will be discussed later in this book.

It is a common ritual in many cultures, especially of the Native-American Indian tribes, to send a young adult out to the unknown land beyond the village, draw a circle or drop a rope in a ten-foot diameter circle, and leave the young adult there alone with a just a canteen of water until he or she has a vision of what he or she should have as their life mission (Harner et al. 1990). Whether it is in a dream, a vision, or some other mode of communication, the young adult arrives back in the camp with an answer. More often than not, the imagery or actual experience is with a totem animal and it is that animal spirit and its attributes of strengths and talents that enable the individual to deal with challenges. For example, if a wolf visits and selects to become the animal spirit, the natural characteristics of close team worker, family networker, compassionate caregiver, and powerful and clever hunter. The young tribesperson then dances the dance of the wolf and dresses in the costume in honor of the wolf in ritual and thus begins a new life with the wolf spirit as his or her source of wisdom, guidance, and protection.

Sensory Deprivation

A session in the sensory deprivation chamber involves the patient being placed in an environment where they are free from all external distractions, leaving them with only the voices, images, and feelings from within. The theory reflects the fact that most people develop their personalities and behaviors in sharp reaction, either in dependence on or in rebellion to, their parents and family. This source of motivation could well be one of the "selves" encased in a personality, as described by Carl Jung (1976), John Lilly (1977), and a number of other psychologists. One of these selves is determined to fit into a social network for survival and develops a persona for this benefit. This self, considered the immortal one, develops into the destiny the person is intent on becoming and serving to the greatest good, based on his skills and talents.

At Origins Recovery Center in South Padre Island, Texas, a sensory deprivation chamber was built for this purpose. The structure created a light-proof boundary and within it placed a water bed mattress with a lamb's wool comforter for tactile deprivation while piping in underneath the chamber a drumming rhythm at a very low level to mask any noise from within and to stimulate the theta brain wave cycles.

For the addicted patients, remarkable results have been seen in their realization of "spirituality" with only fifteen to sixty minutes in duration. Many patients remarked that they discovered forgiveness for themselves, especially around Step Seven in the Twelve Step process. However, the lasting impression is the discovery that they are aware of a spiritual personal self who gives them comfort, guidance, strength, and integrity throughout their days. Most important is they learn how to communicate with this internal wisdom and make decisions for life and change, even to the point of accountability.

Destruction of Myths That Were Obstacles to Life Paths

Probably the most interesting of observations have been in response to the moment when a person's cluster of myths are exposed and challenged. That is the real gift of television psychologist Dr. Phil in which people seem to grasp the reality quite quickly with his blunt style of delivery. Of course, Dr. Phil's words don't exactly sound like those of a monk; however, significant changes have seen its effectiveness in shifting damaging perspectives time and time again. One of the most frequent stories from addicted patients is the scenario of early myths given by families or other important influencers. These often amount to a hex and usually sound something like, "You will never be anything but a bum/whore/loser/piece of s___/failure." Even worse are the myths that convey false accusations and guilt, like "You caused your sister to die or you are the cause of all your mother's suffering."

The removal of these myths can be momentous in freeing the addict to be transformed from an evil doer into a person worthy of feeling joy and being free of guilt and shame, especially mythical guilt. Dr. Stephen Levine (2009) has pointed out that during near-death experiences, there is the stage of forgiveness and letting go of the past, which would be very critical to transformational release. Dr. Kenneth Ring (1982) has also observed in his collection of reports that people with these experiences undergo a connection directly to a wholly spiritual existence, such as being one with the universe, being supported completely by God, or even being engulfed "into the soup of love."

Fortunately, we don't always have to come that close to death to realize the instance of transformation. In many cases, simply being confronted with our mortality can be motivation enough to cause a major myth set transformation. As discussed previously, stories in reality that are consistent with Dickens's *A Christmas Carol* (2009) and Scrooge's nightmares/visions into his own destiny are enough to cause some kind of impact on how one sees their life and their current myth clusters.

There are a number of reports that indicate that altered states of consciousness bring about vivid imagery so powerful to the level of effecting total life transformation. Certain developmental stage rituals have been used along with the similar steps in transformation in order to create the radical shifts presumed with age-specific changes in life; such as marriage, adulthood, retirement, specific anniversaries, child births, and so on. Along with these aspects, rituals are accompanied by physical and psychological demands that often break down resistance to transformation and open the channels to accepting profound life change. Some prime examples are listed below:

- Sensory deprivation
- Solitary confinement from social contact
- Extreme boredom
- Shamanic trances and visions
- Deep relaxation, Hypnosis, Suggestibility
- Hypoglycemia/ Hyperglycemia
- Dehydration

- Sleep deprivation
- Hyperventilation

TWELVE STEPS IN TRANSFORMATION FOR ADDICTION

The steps in addiction transformation as an outline for a course of action for recovery was originally proposed by Bill Wilson and the first one hundred alcoholics who had recovered and was published in the book *Alcoholics Anonymous* in 1939. It has been the basis for many programs combating a variety of addictions. The steps were written as follows (Alcoholics Anonymous 1976):

1. We admitted we were powerless over alcohol—that our lives had become unmanageable.
2. Came to believe that a Power greater than ourselves could restore us to sanity.
3. Made a decision to turn our will and our lives over to the care of God as we understood Him.
4. Made a searching and fearless moral inventory of ourselves.
5. Admitted to God, to ourselves, and to another human being the exact nature of our wrongs.
6. We were entirely ready to have God remove all these defects of character.
7. Humbly asked Him to remove our shortcomings.
8. Made a list of all persons we had harmed, and became willing to make amends to them all.
9. Made direct amends to such people whenever possible, except when to do so would injure them or others.
10. Continued to take personal inventory, and when we were wrong promptly admitted it.
11. Sought through prayer and meditations to improve our conscious contact with God as we understood Him, praying only for knowledge of His will for us and the power to carry that out.
12. Having had a spiritual awakening as the result of these steps, we tried to carry this message to alcoholics, and to practice these principles in all our affairs.

These steps are basis for life change or transformation and are the most utilized by fellowships with a focus on addictions. They have been proclaimed as one with the highest potential for success. These programs all over the world with the same message make it clear that the process can be the same regardless of where you are. It appears obvious that a major ingredient of therapeutic support is the mutual language and understanding within this organization. There is a strong identification with the people as they embrace and care unconditionally with the awareness of their commitment to the central program.

It is also noteworthy that there is tremendous love and respect that is communicated through this fellowship. Serving as a linkage to the belief in the healing of love, the Twelve Steps not only convey content but also a standard ritual of caring and expression that cannot be measured and are obviously a strong feature within the walls of AA. However, rituals themselves have tremendous power for providing safety and assurance of acceptance and can be quantified to prove the importance of the structure of the therapeutic elements contained within.

THE PSYCHONEUROPLASTICITY ASPECTS OF TRANSFORMATION

As the story of Frederick unfolded, it became evident that his transformation process was met with some obstacles, mainly the inability to overcome his negative self-image as a loser who's unworthy of love. Although it would not hurt as a first step to admit defeat over the substance, these self-messages would certainly play a big part in the second step, where he must be willing to assume there was a supreme being who cared about him. For a person who has no self-value, this assumption would be very hard to believe. Moreover, the challenge of being overwhelmed by stress and anxiety would provoke some difficult mental gymnastics as Frederick took inventory of himself and who could assume he could really face those people for whom he should make amends if he didn't have self-confidence to make any functional approach. He obviously had no self-confidence with which he could muster any other scenario than making a mess of any attempt to look normal.

It is little wonder that most of the patients evaluated discuss their drug behavior as self-medicating their psychological problems, such as the "alpha seekers" who use sedatives (pot, heroin, alcohol, etc.) and "beta seekers" who use drugs to get high stimulation (Adderall, cocaine, meth, etc.).

There is sufficient evidence that people who suffer from addiction don't feel very normal to begin with before their addiction, so getting sober may resolve some better mental functioning, but it doesn't erase the problems that were present in the initial stages. In fact, if a person started drugs when they were twelve years old, they missed those important adolescent adjustment skills and when sober, they return to that state of being twelve years old again. Once their brain is detoxed, they have to start to catch up cognitively. One of the most frequent recommendations made when they come into the treatment program and are administered the Minnesota Multiphasic Personality Inventory (MMPI) is "training for social skills."

There are two major destruction zones that are usually present in the recovery process; the damage from the substance disease and the destructive neurological pathways that can occur before or during recovery. The gap between those two arenas of therapeutic efforts and true recovery dictates the relapse of the individual.

It would be a Herculean task for one person to approach all the complexes of a patient. Not only would he or she attempt to tackle the addiction itself, but the knotty personal history and personality of the complex matrix of conflicts and self-perception errors inherent in each of the thousands of stories. Indeed, there are few methods that could even approach the resolutions for one therapist. It takes a village with a team spirit to make a difference.

As one would also acknowledge, these complicated personality problems might need years of therapy by themselves. Frederick is not going to be converted from his depressions and anxieties with the goodwill of an inspiring confrontation or a threat of someone who foresees relapse. A 30-day program may not be able to touch these areas and a 90-day program might not either. Any psychology textbook will grant that truth.

As initiated earlier, it is the brain's faulty perceptions and wave forms that can be changed rather than the attitudes and learned behavior of years. It is the new field of *neuroplasticity* that has emerged in the last three years that is changing our whole notion of change in potential. Also explained in the next chapter in detail, neuroplasticity is the ability of the brain to make new pathways, to create new brain cells, and to find new avenues for function. For example, a man who has suffered a brain trauma that wiped out one side of his brain can function normally again once the brain creates new avenues of connections on the other side. A woman can learn to talk again even though her speech centers were wiped out with a stroke. A professor can return to his teaching position again because his memory banks were reprogrammed internally. There are thousands of examples that have medical evidence of this huge capacity to restore cognitive and physical function.

The same principles pertain to psychological states, hence the additional label of *PsychoNeuroPlatsicity* or PNP. As demonstrated on *The Dr. Phil Show* and *The Doctors* television shows, major phobias can be managed in as quickly as forty minutes. PTSD can be conquered in a day. Depression can be lifted in twenty minutes. And these changes are permanent. These specific avenues have been explained in Dr. Lawlis's *Retraining the Brain* (2009); however, they were not applied to addiction. But it is the intention of this book to describe these techniques for the addiction recovery process specifically.

THE PSYCHOLOGICAL/NEUROLOGICAL
OBSTACLES TO TRANSFORMATION

Several years ago an imagery exercise was created for patients who were facing major disease issues in their lives, such as cancer, MS, Lupus, and chronic pain, for the purpose of dealing with obstacles they would face for a transformative process (Lawlis, *Imagery Journey into Transformation*, unpublished manuscript). Universal symbols were used to signify their challenges, such as a deep river that represented the depth of their habitual behaviors that they would have to change; a great wall symbolizing the self-inflicted rules they kept in their minds that immobilized them; and a giant representing the authority they would have to ignore if they wanted to change for themselves. It was a success for those few therapists who understood the use of imagery and could translate the subtle underlying dynamics of the process.

Most of the basics are evident in the history of life events, their family history, and relationship problems. The top five obstacles have been selected to discuss in terms of PNP applications that are amendable to the approaches and the patients see the immediate implications for them in their lives.

The An-Type Obstacle

The most frequent category, according to our numbers, are the patients who suffer from anxiety issues, the An-type obstacles. These are the patients whose EEG brain scans show their brains are running very fast, too fast to be able to focus on any one thing long enough to find resolutions to any problem, similar to a car with a motor running at 100 miles per hour that can't stop to buy gas. Another subtype of the An-type obstacle is the person whose brain is running fast but in circles, similar to Obsessive Compulsive Disorder, so there is constant illogical circulating on the same problem with no solutions. Common issues seen are patients who wonder repeatedly why their parents didn't love them the way they should, always feeling deprived and asking why.

Leslie was a client that fit this description perfectly. She was constantly thinking and would complain of her mind acting faster than the words she could get out of her mouth. Leslie was tearful when she got to the facility, complaining of her anxiety being so monumental that she could not stand to feel this way and wanted to leave to get relief with her drug of choice. Leslie also felt that she could not get along with the community because she felt like she was constantly being judged or watched under a microscope. The anxiety would try to get the best of her.

The D-Type Obstacle

The second obstacle, which overlaps with the anxiety issue, is the depressed patient, similar to some of Frederick's issues. Their brain maps are usually running slower than normal overall but have high and low frequencies in specific areas. They are most often low in the temporal and frontal areas, which relate to reasoning and emotional issues. There is often ruminating thoughts about messages kept over the years that keep the patient in a box of expectations, such as "You aren't ever going to amount to anything but a piece of s___," "You are going to turn out just like your Uncle Rick," and others that pervade a person's self-worth and ultimately their destiny. Of course, these statements don't have to be external; they can also be self-statements created some time later in life. There are also biological reasons for their unhappiness. For example, some addicted people's pleasure centers have been found to be low functioning for a long period of their lives and drugs may be the first time they have felt "normal." A common diagnostic category for these individuals has been referred to as "dysthymia." Another subtype is the people whose anxieties and their lack of control lead to depression, so that they feel overrun with fears and failures. These types would be seen as "agitated depressive syndrome."

A prime example of this is Joel who grew up in a family that did not show any type of emotion. This robotic family life style was his message, and he felt that if he showed emotion it would be considered weak. Joel kept all his emotions bottled up and grew up to be a depressed man revealing little words or affect. Joel was never able to attain lasting relationships since he kept other people at a shallow level. The message Joel stored in his cognitions was "You do not deserve to show emotion." Joel displayed the robotic energy he learned from his family when he arrived to Origins.

And becoming more frequent are the PTSD patients who have yet to find their internal compass in life and their brains are under no control. They have rage as their anxieties roam from situation to situation and depression in their functional dimensions because their brains are damaged from biological, psychological, and spiritual realities.

Mark was a veteran that lived with daily nightmares that haunted him even in the day time. He admitted that he did not know how to cope with these daily reminders that screamed to him that he was a lost person in the world. Mark needed coping skills and, even more, a purpose for living. Mark showed his frustration through anger and on his third day of treatment he ended up breaking a couple pieces of furniture because of his rage. Beneath the rage, was a man that was sad and worn out from the stress he had in his brain.

The Acc-Obstacle

This obstacle is likely listed as the primary early age addiction development called the acculturated obstacle to recovery transformation. This type is the typical scenario in which the kid is exposed to drugs at an early stage and goes into the habit as a function of "everyone else is doing it." As they sober, they are still at the age in which they started using and their attitudes are not much different. They still think that drugs are the mode of the average citizen and the prediction of going back to the same crowd is typically the case. While it is hard to resocialize a person at this stage, there are PNP methods that can be useful and powerful.

Annie's parents died at a young age and she found her new family to be the community on the streets. Her grandma would attempt to rescue her but did not have the energy or money to act this out properly. Annie was left to learn about drugs and prostitution from an early age. Her compass was set for survival and methods to continue her drug life style. It was easy to tell when she came to treatment that she was juvenile and her attitude did not match her actual age, even dressing as a teenage girl. Annie had quite a bit of adjusting to do when she came to Origins because she now had more than enough to survive—food, shelter, and the human connection; she had enough to thrive and this concept was very new to her.

The V-Self Obstacle

Mostly found among women is the Vacant Self Obstacle. The typical story is a girl being brought up by her family as a sexual object and no more. As any therapist would predict, they have been the victim of molestation sexually, morally, psychologically, and spiritually. By the way, children that have been neglected through overprotective parents creating their lives for them and never allowing them to fail can be classified in this category. As a result they never had the opportunity to know who they are and what boundaries they might have. Without a guide of a self-concept, even one that is negative, all they have is to wander through life. Drugs may be the only reality they have for any sense of achievement.

Tori was subjected to this classification and her history matches the V-Self Obstacle completely. From a young age, she learned how to shoot up heroin from her father who used her as his sexual pawn. Tori had to start from scratch when she came to our facility; "Who am I?" was a question that she was faced with on a daily basis. Like Annie, Tori was also cognitively delayed in her growth and presented as younger than her actual age.

The I-Obstacle

Perhaps the saddest cases are those patients who have been impaired by drug abuse so that their cognitive abilities resemble a stroke victim. Easily detected through neurological function tests, such as memory and problem-solving skills, their brains have been withered to the point of limited potentials and have very little capacity to earn the kind of lives they would enjoy. This is not a newsflash to them or their families, but until now there has been no protocol for them. They can't catch on to the principles taught for transformation, yet they often have the best neuroplasticity factors. There are new PNP protocols that have great benefit for these individuals and have raised the hope toward a fruitful life.

Jake spent the majority of his life lifting weights and competing in "strong man competitions." Jake found steroids and came to find out this magnified his results in the gym. He did not just stop at steroids and his addiction sprawled out of control as began trying everything and anything he could get his hands on. Of course, his fitness training stopped and his new passion became drug use. Jake found himself in and out of treatment twelve times. Jake arrived and the cognitive damage through the years was obvious. He struggled with formulating sentences and staying on the right track when he was speaking. Jake found PNP protocols to be significant for him and was overwhelmed with happiness when he found his brain being stimulated while interacting with these protocols.

There are other classifications that are less numerous but deserve some special thought, such as the tremendous surge of medically prescribed medication addictions growing larger each year, such as pain, anxiety, ADHD, depression, and weight control drugs. These require a different mindset that is similar to transformational processes, yet they all have the same obstacles. Please refer to appendix C for a checklist of PNP approaches to barriers such as these that block someone from getting sober with the Twelve Steps.

SUMMARY

This book is based in science, love, and a faith in the potential of humankind to rise to the spirit with the true sense of recovery. There is a minor resistance to use the term "rehabilitation" because its definition means to return to the same state of functioning as before an event of injury or trauma. Transformation has a more powerful meaning in that the individual becomes better off than they were before such an event. He or she has greater capacities and more potential because they have been given a gift of strength and power over their lives that they never had before. They may be damaged, but they are not disabled from engaging in a new life that is truly converted into a richer life without the barriers of their early obstacles. There is no basis for our expectations on theory but on the realities of seeing individuals blossoming in front of their family and friends' eyes, and seeing them experiencing their own gifts for the very first time. It is this mode of transformation which contains the power to heal the addicted person and which sets them free to begin a new life with untold potential.

THREE

The Principles of Psychoneuroplasticity

Dating back to the Dark Ages (AD 500–1000) it was generally believed that mental illnesses of the mind and body were either caused by demons or were punishments for one's sinful behaviors. Addiction was not considered a part of health but a clear sign of lack of will and self-centered gratification, that is, laziness. The possibility of being possessed by the devil led to many "witch hunts" to expose the wickedness within.

Enter the significance of Sigmund Freud (and his followers) in the early 1900s, a psychiatrist with great ambitions to make the mind a science. His group of psychoanalytic researchers created mythical brain patterns based on patients who suffered brain trauma and their associated behaviors. Notably his concepts of id, ego, and superego could not be traced to a topology of the brain, but they served to be a common terminology for professionals and journalists to discuss with one another.

The field became disenchanted when this "psychoanalysis" talk therapy failed to further the scientific quest, and further exploration went into personality theory built to a great extent on using psychometric methodology to project into the mind's dimensions. The MMPI and 16 personality factors (PF) emerged as the most empirical products and are still used as valid estimates of the states of the brain as to pathology.

Neuro-chemistry has pushed the exploration to new heights as neurotransmitters were discovered and the labs were destined to correlate mind states and changes to actual brain fluids and neurological patterns. This development excited the medical world because pills became an inexpensive option to talk therapies. However, to a large extent most of these remedies fail to actually change brain patterns, but mostly to either numb the person from reacting to the surges of pathological anxieties and depressions or stimulating the neurological into addictive patterns, which have the danger of making the life experience worse. This era has yet to see its full results on the public. The health issues of prescribed medications for pain, anxiety, lack of concentration, and depression are becoming more of a social problem than cocaine and heroin put together.

Although the psychiatric view appears to have met the challenge to bring the study of the mind up to the standards of the rest of medical science, the precision of diagnosis of mental disorders is far from its objectives in terms of success in even understanding the problems, much less understanding the wellness dimensions that is our real goal in this field. The metaphor seems apt of the intensity of understanding cancer as a disease without understanding the immune system as a cure.

MEDICAL APPROACH TODAY AND BEYOND

Think about the current process when you go to a medical professional for help. Suppose one has a stomachache and explains the pain to a doctor. After taking a medical history and conducting a physical exam, the doctor (hopefully) sends you for x-rays and blood tests, perhaps stool samples and other related assessments. In the final analysis, the process would be to *triangulate* the results, that is, to ascertain how the clinical signs fit the lab results to determine diagnosis and choose the best treatment.

However, if one goes to a doctor for mental stress issues, there aren't tests to triangulate, because one can't see thoughts on x-rays, and there's no identifiable virus or bacteria for stress. What an individual will likely experience is a set of questions that has symptoms of stress and some behavioral discontent. This process may take five minutes and one has a diagnosis and lists of medication pertaining to that label which has just been assigned. Thus, the "proper" or "best" course of treatment up to this point has been educated guesswork. However, exciting advancements in technology are changing all that. Scientists are now finding ways to see a thought—or at least the process of a thought—which can help medical professionals triangulate a diagnosis.

BRAIN LANGUAGING

In addition to the technology revolution, there is another revolution going on. The second and arguably even more revolutionary breakthrough is the advent of a concept called *brain plasticity* (also called neuroplasticity). This field of research has demonstrated that (contrary to popular belief) the brain isn't permanently hardwired by the age of five, but rather, is able to physically, chemically, and anatomically change in response to thoughts, experiences, and behaviors throughout a lifetime. This suggests that humans can alter—and therefore potentially heal—the brain by directing the organization of stress thoughts (e.g., through mental training) in a step-by-step method!

Today, our medical culture has a set of evaluations and diagnostic tools that are not unlike what other forms of medicine have been using for many years. Professionals can evaluate and measure the degree of healing. They can triangulate which protocols will serve best to optimize quality of life. This is possibly as great a leap forward in public health as discovering antibiotics and vaccines.

Before the brain can be fully understood, it's important to define what "normalcy" is and what optimal brain functioning is, which starts with brain geography. The geography of the brain's outermost layer is the cerebral cortex—which is in charge of voluntary actions, thinking, memory, feelings, and conscious experience; it will give you a good overall understanding of this three-pound wonder, otherwise known as our brain.

There are several distinct regions of the cerebral cortex—the organizational divisions— which are usually associated with the demands placed on us in terms of being successful in life. In figure 3.1, these general areas are defined. For example, when people are injured or have lesions in the parietal lobe (the voluntary movement/motor and sensory section), there's a specific correlation to a function in the body. More specifically, if one suffered a certain type of stroke in the left parietal area, he or she would likely experience paralysis in the right arm or leg. Why? Nearly all the nerve signals from the brain to the body cross over both coming and going. The left cerebral hemisphere controls the right side of your body, and vice versa. But contrary to popular belief, being left or right handed doesn't signify which side of your brain is "dominant."

Encouragingly, as discussed earlier, your brain can and does adapt. This is possible because, while each part of the brain has its own special functions and properties, they also have the capacity to influence other parts. In other words, the brain is like a board of experts who come together to optimize the company (which is the person) as an integrated whole.

BRAIN PROCESSES, IN BRIEF

- Prefrontal lobe: Responsible for integrating information and organizing our perceptions into meaningful concepts. People with prefrontal lobe injuries often have difficulty organizing new information and appear to be in a daze. The prefrontal lobe plays a critical role in memory retrieval.
- Frontal lobe: Responsible for planning, reasoning, judgment, and impulse control, as well as some aspects of speech. People who

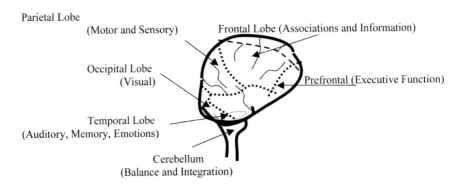

Parietal Lobe
        (Motor and Sensory)   Frontal Lobe (Associations and Information)

Occipital Lobe
        (Visual)   Prefrontal (Executive Function)

Temporal Lobe
(Auditory, Memory, Emotions)

                Cerebellum
            (Balance and Integration)

Figure 3.1.   A Function-Related Map of the Brain

have problems in this lobe frequently are impulsive and have very poor planning skills.

- Temporal lobe: Responsible for auditory processing (hearing), comprehension of words and emotional affect in context with language. People with low functioning temporal lobes also exhibit memory problems.
- Parietal lobe: Responsible for processing sensations such as touch, pressure, cold, heat, and pain. It also has an integration process that takes data from language, symbols, and other data and makes sense of it. It's also strongly involved with primary motor functions (voluntary movements). People with limitations in this area often have trouble controlling their body and lose sensations (touch, smell, etc.), as in some cases of strokes and traumatic head injuries.
- Occipital lobe (visual cortex): Responsible for processing and interpreting data provided by the eyes into meaningful symbols. People with damaged occipital lobes may become blind, even when their eyes are functioning well.
- Cerebellum: Responsible for balance, posture and coordination as well as learned physical skills, such as riding a bike. Cerebellum is also Latin for "little brain" as it must coordinate millions of impulses instantaneously; else, you'd constantly be falling down.

TECHNOLOGY AND THE BRAIN

QEEG Activity

A QEEG (quantitative electroencephalograph) is a type of brain mapping diagnostic tool that takes the electronic impulses from the brain regions and displays how the brain's regions are performing in terms of frequency ranges, which can illustrate what may be happening at cross-purposes. For example, in the case of a person with high anxiety, the QEEG brain scan probably would show too much High Beta frequency in the frontal lobe and an overall imbalance in regards to the rest of the brain regions. This is an indicator of anxiety, similar to a machine that is running too fast for the rest of the brain to catch up. The signature of high electronic activity is reliable and its treatment protocol is clear: the treatment program would likely include techniques that will moderate the abnormally high frequencies in the frontal lobe to more efficient ones in concert with the rest of the brain.

The SPECT scan (Single Photon Emission Computed Tomography) is a type of nuclear imaging test that demonstrates how blood flows through arteries and veins in the brain and where blockages or reduced blood flow is occurring. This is particularly helpful because highly active regions usually produce less active areas and receive less blood flows, which are indications of injury or problems.

In the case of the attention deficit hyperactivity disorder (ADHD) signature, the SPECT scan would likely show the frontal lobes are less active and, therefore, would show less blood flow than normal. Overly high blood flow might suggest that the areas are overactive or inflamed, which would be cause for a treatment plan to reduce blood flow.

SUMMARIZING THE IMPLICATIONS

This is the most valuable new technology that exists for identifying problems and determining troubled areas. As discussed earlier, diagnoses to this point have been based primarily on the art of mental health—along with the sensitivities to find the most important and relevant behaviors on which to base a diagnosis. This takes years of skill and training, as

Table 3.1
Recognized States of Consciousness to Brain Frequencies (Lawlis 2008)

Frequencies	Name	State of consciousness
0.5 – 4 Hz.	Delta	Sleep/Subconscious/total internal processing
4 – 8 Hz.	Theta	Fantasy/Dreamy/ Semiconscious
8 – 12	Alpha	Little information being learned/High memory
12 – 15	SMR or LoBeta	Focused/Studying/ Processing external data
15 +	High Beta	Anxious/Overwhelmed/Little concentration

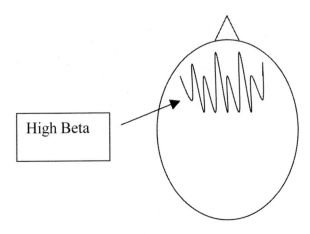

Figure 3.2.   Associated Brain Signature to Anxiety

there can be a multitude of diagnostic categories that are contributing to a problem and it's not always accurate. Further, not only is data reliability an issue, the diagnostic categories can be confusing. These categories are defined (and redefined) periodically by a committee of known experts and are published for the field in Diagnostic and Statistical Manuals (DSM) (American Psychiatric Association 2000).

With the technological advancement of brain mapping, scientists and laymen alike can finally get a leg up. Professionals and patients can now talk to each other in real terms, on a more level playing field, and reliability can be attained with a scientific foundation established for all.

This is an amazing feat. No longer are professionals left with only the best guess about what's going on in the brain. People can begin the process of changing the functioning of the brain and modifying the organizational abilities (brain plasticity). For example, the military has been studying the problems of understanding the effects of Post Traumatic Syndrome for years, and now it can be evaluated in its process over time and determine best treatment protocols for it. Individuals can be taught better prevention practices as professionals understand the disease components better and can develop specific treatment protocols for efficient evaluation as well as direct impact on the brain dynamics.

CHANGING THE PATTERNS ON PURPOSE

Brain plasticity is truly at the frontier in understanding human nature—a grand and glorious mystery. With its amazing array of intricate fibers and endless connections, the processing of the brain reduces even the most brilliant of scientists to the humble admission that there is not a clue

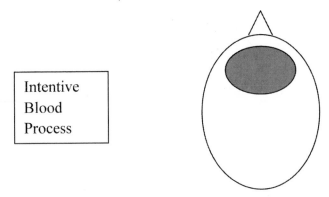

Intentive
Blood
Process

Figure 3.3. Associated ADD Map

how to replicate even its smallest of functions. More sophisticated than our best computers, the brain can *simultaneously* calculate 10^{24} bits of information? That gargantuan number is a 10 with 24 zeroes behind it!

As much as scientists are closer to understanding how humans think and feel, understanding is still rather primitive when it comes to knowing how exactly the brain actually equips humans to do the incredibly complex tasks they do as a matter of living life. For example, the brain coordinates everything from walking, sleeping, solving complex problems, enjoying a sunset and bike riding. Humans are able to make sense from hundreds of thousands of sound vibrations; humans perceive and understand millions of light waves coming into our retinas and understand our world. People interpret the world around them and develop a sense of values and justice that helps them live together.

Yet, humans are not alike in the brain and certain abilities are pronounced in different people. There are confusing similarities and differences that sometimes go counter to our survival. Thus, the question enters the possibility that these differences could be explained in brain chemistries, and if found abnormal, could be retracted to normalcy. The purpose of this manual is to equip professionals to help individuals to have the ability to not only discover, but also invent who they are and who they can become. Professionals simply need to bring together the will and the way.

THE FRONTIER AWAITS

It helps to take a quick look at the journey of brain plasticity from its rudimentary beginnings to appreciate how far it has come. A brilliant, pioneering brain surgeon and researcher named Dr. Wilder Penfield created the first "brain maps" that are still used today. He used simple electrical probes to gently stimulate different parts of the brain to see what behavior would happen (Penfield and Jasper 1954). For example, he probably discovered the motor strip function by stimulating the top of a subject's head and an arm would fly up. Likely he probed another area on the other side and the other leg would turn. His subjects would be fully conscious during these procedures making it possible for the subjects to tell him what they were experiencing. For example, he might have touched a certain part of the temporal lobe, and the subject might start to cry or laugh. Another spot might stimulate the visions of various symbols or sounds.

It is interesting that Dr. Penfield investigated many brains and never said that all brain maps were identical for every human being, but there are those who have historically insisted this is the case. The brain is much more mysterious than that assertion. For example, it is now known that while the language region is located in the brain's left hemisphere in about 95 percent of right-handed people, the language region is located in the right hemisphere for a portion of left-handers.

Brain plasticity is newly recognized as scientific, evidence-based fact, although it is still foreign to many scientists. Although known for fifty years, the brain has an amazing capacity for instituting functional backup systems that can renew lost functions. More current research has shown that if the brain comes to an impasse, *it can literally grow alternate routes.* This is like having a team of people who not only have cross training abilities, but are also experts at constructing workable detours, meaning if one person gets sick, another can do his job without shutting down the whole factory. Someday humans may have the ability to rewire their brain so they telecommute without going through their verbal abilities.

For those patients with weakened or damaged psychological or cognitive functions, accessing their brain's flexibility opens up a whole new world of possibilities. This includes the brain of a person who has suffered a stroke that damaged the motor regions of the brain. There have actually been some cases in which people have re-taught their brains to use their legs to walk after massive damage to the basic areas learned at birth. Individuals who have suffered strokes and damage their neural networks in finding their balance have retreaded other areas to take over those abilities.

In addiction cases, the brain is usually injured by toxicity or stress. They forget how to care for themselves psychologically and biologically. But the discovery of the hidden treasures of what the mind can do for them, if allowed to relearn, is vast. And since humans are always remodeling the brain throughout life, these are within the reach of rediscovery.

From a neuro-chemical perspective, good and bad behaviors are the same thing. Both result from the interplay of our neural networks. But neurological reflexes and pathways can be relearned, which means the brain and our intentions can fix things. The "fixing" part of the equation

is a two-part process which means a retraining or replacement of the pathways that are destructive and the reinstallation of the positive, helpful pathways wanted. A professional is needed to assist to teach the brain what a patient desires in their lives.

BRAIN PLASTICITY PRINCIPLES

There are multiple principles to brain plasticity and five have been found that underlie most of what is known about people who are successful in changing their lives. These are simple enough and behind each principle is the founding truth—practice.

Principle I

> *Brain neurons that learn together become attached in bundles.* (Lawlis, F. 2009)

This principle merely states that brain neurons that fire together, wire together. The latest technological advances have clearly shown the more two or more neural conduits share common frequency patterns, that when they can combine into common activities, including thinking patterns. This is the very basis for habit formation. It's also the basis for coordination of body components, such as muscles and organs. Psychologically, people teach their brains from associating their thinking and behavior. In EEG terms, when there are similarities in frequency wave forms, they are called "coherence" patterns. This is measured in a term of correlation from -1.00 (opposite predictable action) to +1 (predictable in the same direction). In figure 3.4 below, the two neuro-patterns are correlated at 0.99—which is an impressively high coherence number.

An example would be the correlation of when a person drinks too much alcohol and the psychological sensation is a disconnection to worries and urgency. As the strength of coherence between these two events occurs, the power of that connection grows stronger and overwhelming. As the neurological pathways merge, they also collect others, which build and refine as they develop the most efficient pathways by disposing of intermittent steps, such as judgment and consequences. This process will continue to build neurological strength as long as it is reinforced. Hopefully, the habit being reinforced isn't destructive or counterproductive because breaking those bonds can be a difficult and painful process.

Principle II

> *Neurological bundles are changed according to experience and evolved need.* (Lawlis, F. 2009)

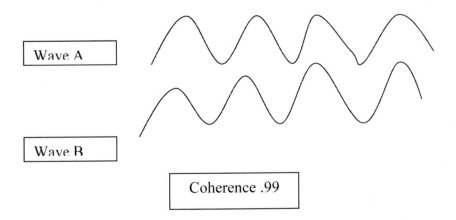

Figure 3.4. Coherence Model

There are three processes that are basic to all brain plasticity. The first is dispersion or disruption, which might take place in our nerve patterns during assimilating new information. As any addiction counselor knows, it is exceedingly difficult to break habits neurologically or behaviorally merely by announcing a desire to do so. For example, smokers will attest to the experience of consistently meeting failure when attempting to break the smoking habit. Similarly, it's difficult to stop overreacting to an angry person when in conflict, or to stop obsessively worrying about our children when there has so many reinforcing years of practice. But thinking and behavior habits can be changed. A common way for people to stop a habit is by asking friends or family to "call them out" and catch them while they are in action so they can stop. This is an example of common-sense thinking and considered disruption of the habit or action that they want to end.

Principle III

> With the suspension of thoughts or the elimination of specific experiences, there is immediate availability for reformation of neurological networks and transformation. (Lawlis, F. 2009)

Dr. Michael Merzenich has championed brain plasticity with his foundational research. From his work it is now known that when a function is eliminated or diminished, even a thought pattern, the neurological networks of other functions will grab the newly available space and incorporate the extra storage into their areas. Like a glass filled with water that has one ice cube, the moment the ice cube is removed, the water fills in the available space. Brain neurons compete for space (and attention) in similar ways.

One of the outstanding experiments that Dr. Merzenich conducted was to assess the behavior cluster of neurons that activated a monkey's right hand middle finger (Merzenich et al. 1984). He amputated this finger, and waited a period of time to assess how the neurons would react. When he evaluated the brain neurons he found that although the middle finger neurons had disappeared with the surgery, the neuron clusters from the adjoining fingers had taken over. The results were like other research with patients who lost the function of hearing through trauma; those patients often develop other skills, such as increased visual acuity. The monkey would have developed compensating abilities in those fingers left.

These implications have enormous ramifications. If a person had a stroke and could no longer use a preferred hand, practicing with the other hand long enough would result in a heightened ability to learn to write or throw with the other hand. There are many examples of people who relearn how to talk and listen from completely different parts of the original brain neuro-clusters. In similar ways, a person can learn new habits in dealing with anxiety other than depending on drugs.

Changing emotional sets work along this same principle. For example, if a person has always used aggressive behavior to express his rage, he can be taught to express it with optional word vocabulary and alternative behavior that will resolve his emotional conflicts more effectively, that is, he can learn to react differently. A parent can learn not to scream at his or her children in a futile attempt to gain control of their behavior. A boss can learn better ways of "motivating" his workers rather than using harsh words and fear tactics. In spite of the myth, old dogs *can* learn new tricks if one knows how to change the brain patterns.

Principle IV

Learning and relearning are growth factors. (Lawlis, F. 2009)

The processing of the brain is not consistent forever, nor is it changing in a linear fashion. It depends on the opportunities for growth and the availability for change. People start out in life with a potential for thinking and understanding life, but the brain changes with critical events. Sometimes it is a trauma that destroys faith in self. Sometimes it can be a revelation of truth that can create new hope in change.

This appears to be self-evident. Learning in the brain, whether for motor skills or emotions, is not a mysterious process. It starts and stops rather abruptly with the correlation of some biochemical dispersion of brain growth factors (Cohen, S., Levi-Montalcini, R., & Hamburger, V. (1954). It becomes clear that brain growth factors turn on the nucleus basalis and coat each neuron with a rich, fatty substance that "lubricates" it and speeds up the learning process exponentially. But it doesn't stay turned on forever: When this process shuts down, the whole system slows back to a stable pace. The question of why it slows down abruptly has to do with lack of attention and positive reinforcement perhaps. This principle makes it clear that learning of the brain is based on times of opportunity, but to a certain extent, the opportunity can be under a person's circumstances and even created.

Intention and Attention

A professional counselor's concern is how to turn this process on. In the plasticity of the brain, attention and intention are vital to the critical stages of learning or relearning. Unfortunately, one can't learn much without trying or being motivated. The truth is, although technically the brain is always awake, that process has to have a person's intention or attention to create the necessary neuron networks. In addiction the occasion has to be created in a rehab program and one cannot wait around for the opportunity for growth to occur out of the blue.

Plus, not only does mobilization of nerve pathways have to have clear intention, there has to have a neurological excitement about what a person is doing. This emotional edge is what provides the vitality to open up the door to real change. Being emotionally invested helps get the brain to be prepped to meet the challenges or intentions.

Interestingly, many foods have been implicated in increasing learning curves, but this should not be too surprising since many of us learned our basic toilet training through food rewards. High protein (as in eggs and meat), Omega 3 and 10 (as in fish), and some complex carbohydrates have some pretty meaningful impact on the brain. It was known in the 1920s that a high "good" fat diet with low sugar helps repair the brain, so it makes sense that those nutrients would be healthy for brain plasticity and change.

Another very powerful stimulation is musical or rhythmic stimulation, such as singing and drumming. The brain is sensitive to external rhythmic vibrations of any kind, and the frequencies of the brain can be driven with such intention. This is the basics of neurological training and finding the personal sonic stimulation that works for the individual brain can have tremendously positive implications for constructive change.

Principle V

New pathways need to have a positive attitude to make them last. (Lawlis, F. 2009)

Frustration often rears its ugly head when the observation is made of a new behavior, such as absence of drugging, in a person making good, positive choices in stressful situations or moments of conflict, and a month later the old stuff comes flooding back again. This is a problem in therapy. A patient seen once a week has just enough time to go back to the old habits that the objects of treatment were trying to change in the first place. Once the destructive thinking stopped and created a better one, there needs to be stable plasticity.

Repetition of Thinking and Behavior

It takes practice and time for the brain to reorganize itself around newfound insights, generally considered to be six weeks. All the insight mustered in a counseling session won't help an individual create and sustain a new way of life in the absence of practice. A famous golfer was asked how it felt to get paid for playing a hobby. He laughed and replied, "You see me today swinging my club maybe a total of 300 times. What you didn't see was me practicing each shot over 100,000 times during my early training years." The incredible basketball great Michael Jordan would practice shooting the same shot from the same place 10,000 times. This principle merely states the obvious: potential is one attribute, persistence is another.

Everyone has the potential to change his or her brain plasticity but some need coaching. They have to follow a plan, and to make it last, they have to practice. The main principle is that psychoneuroplacity works from the insights out and the real ability to reorganize neuro-networks lies in the inspiration.

Positive Reinforcement and Attention

At the New York Medical Center, Friday mornings usually meant seminars with guest speakers. On one of these mornings in 1968, one of these speakers was named Neal Miller, who walked in and told how he could change the blood flow in one ear of a rat and keep the other ear constant. He called this process "biofeedback." Although the professional application has changed for humans since, the approach has been validated in brain plasticity. This is simply the rule that *you need to enjoy what you're doing in order to establish a brain shift and that enjoyment could be defined psychologically as a positive reinforcement.*

The brain needs to experience joy and happiness in making these changes in order to be fully integrated into the system. Dr. Miller (1978) discussed how he electrically stimulated the "happiness" center whenever the rat behaved in the desired way. Giving treats as rewards stimulates the "happy place" with dogs. One could teach oneself new approaches to life's problems by way of enjoying social acceptance from the family or use tasty treats on oneself.

The problem is that people often forget this important, and very real, cycle. People cram for an exam at the last minute, and in short order, forget everything they ever learned because they didn't add the positive reinforcement necessary for sustainability. People forget, and then make their children learn the multiplication tables without so much as a smile; only utilizing their fear of failure. And people wonder why they can't learn them quicker. The brain opens up to new learning when this powerful approach is used with positive reinforcement and attention.

FOUR

Addiction Pathways and Psychoneuroplasticity

Until fairly recently, addiction was thought of as a behavioral habit that needed to be changed and to do so the addict was expected to simply stop using and the problem would be solved. We now know that addiction is far more complicated than that and is looked at as a disease, which requires a specific treatment protocol to reflect that. Though our current scientific and medical communities are all in agreement on this view of addiction, even to this day there are states such as California with outdated policies stating that no medical care can be given within the walls of an addiction treatment program, and this includes those licensed by the Department of Public Health.

The definition generally accepted in professional treatment programs worldwide states that addiction is an abnormal condition that affects the body in destructive ways and is a "medical condition" associated with specific symptoms and signs. The destructive elements can be internal and external and there are a variety of other breakdowns involved with this disease which has plagued human kind from its earliest known history. This broader understanding realizes that the disease of addiction is not a choice; rather, it is similar to any other disease such as diabetes or cancer. Included in this view is evidence that humans have certain predispositions toward the propensity of acquiring this disease through their genetics, DNA, RNA, and exposures in early life development and family history.

Like other diseases that start with genetic dispositions and carry into disease form, such as a person with a family history of heart disease which is brought to fruition in their bodies by stress and an unbalanced lifestyle, the end result is a disease state whose causes are complex. By making choices early on in life, the formation of these complicated disease forces can potentially be turned around by will and education, but at its victimization stage, full immersive treatment with a medical protocol is needed at the most basic levels.

ADDICTION AS A DISEASE

Addiction is a disease that affects every system in the body including the liver, lungs, and the heart, as well as a plethora of other damages related to the lifestyle of addiction, which include the mental cognitive decline (memory, concentration, etc.), vitamin deficiency, loss of strength, and much more. The deepest damage is centered primarily in the brain. It is not a virus or bacteria, but rather a chronic biological condition that eventually eliminates all reasoning and perpetuates a total breakdown of values and the addict's behavior usually reflects that. Unless checked, the end result is death.

A true addict cannot stop abusing drugs and alcohol, even to save his or her life. Diabetes II is often used as an example to make this point. Often associated with eating too much sugar, a pre-diabetic II can stop eating sugar and perhaps save his health, but once the body has modified itself and metabolism to the point of being labeled with Diabetes II, one is in a disease state that requires constant medical attention and continuous monitoring.

In terms of addiction, there is a boundary between habit and disease based on the presenting patient's brain toxicity and the extent that their destructive behaviors are interfering with their ability to function in life. It starts with drug or alcohol use that becomes a habit that has the potential to become a disease at any point. In some addicts, the disease state may be formed after just one use in that they lose total control over their life and are consumed entirely by the drug from that point on. Some have an inheritance to it and others have a biological connection that leads to addiction. Many times psychological factors play a huge part as a person tries to medicate themselves against their nightmares and anxieties, only to create more than he or she can handle. At this date, no one knows what path a single person will take, and experience has shown that the younger and more rebellious the person starts out, the harder it is for them to make the necessary changes.

What Happens in the Addicted Brain?

Addiction is a disease of the brain and there are very complex neurological destructions concurrently occurring in the brain at the addictive level of functioning. It has recently discovered two little almond-shaped parts of the brain about three inches behind the eyes which are our "pleasure centers" called nucleus accumbens. For most of us, this is where one can take the dopamine and other stimulating juices in our systems and convert them into joyful life experiences. In the 1950s, James Olds and Peter Milner implanted electrodes into this general area of a rat's brain and found that the rat chose to press a lever that stimulated it. They continued to prefer this even over stopping to eat or drink, showing that the electrical stimulation to this area of the brain provided more pleasure than that of fulfilling hunger and thirst (Olds and Milner 1954).

Although the nucleus accumbens have traditionally been studied for their role in addiction, they play an equal role in processing rewards such as food and sex. Interestingly, the nucleus accumbens are selectively activated during the presence of music, sugar-based food, sexual perceptions, and various forms of drugs. For example, cocaine creates one hundred times the arousal of food, while sex creates about three hundred times the arousal. As the nucleus accumbens are activated, emotional memories are triggered and that may explain why cravings can be so powerful for the addict.

For some, especially those diagnosed with ADHD, the nucleus accumbens have been found to be only 50 percent as efficient as average in metabolizing dopamine, which might explain why on brain images this part of the brain that is usually stimulated by the pleasure center (prefrontal cortex) is so minimal (Blum, Chen, Braverman, et al. 2008). Many addicts will say that using stimulants makes them feel "normal" and as happy as others. One could reasonably see why there could be a DNA link to addiction of this nature.

The brain has a wider array of regions involved in addiction than just the nucleus accumbens pleasure centers and professionals are gaining scientifically into the linkages, avenues, and pathways of how the person gets wrapped into the disease of addiction. For instance, Segen Barak and his team of researchers found that just a drop of alcohol presented to rats turned on the mTOPC1 pathway specifically in the region of the amygdala (Barak, Liu, Hamida, Yowell, Neasta, Kharazia, et al. 2013). Once the region was activated the alcohol memory stabilized and the rats started to push a level consistently and obsessively to dispense more drops of alcohol, representing a rat model of craving. The smell and taste were such strong cues that the memory could be targeted without impacting other memories, such as craving for sugar.

The researchers found that they could drug the amygdala to disrupt the memory and the craving behavior ceased; however, the drug would be highly controversial for humans. As will be covered in the later part of this chapter, the sonic stimulation of the Bio Acoustical Utilization Device (BAUD) can also be used to disrupt the amygdala in a safe and self-regulated method. However, it should be clear that the craving is not a critical feature to control; rather, it is the emotional memory that is central to the management of addiction.

THE SLIPPERY SLIDE

As the person becomes more habitual in getting this high from the arousal impact on his or her nucleus accumbens and the memory recoding of the amygdala, the brain is changing its whole process in order to have the pleasure stimulation. Our brain is then focused on what Freud called the "pleasure principle" and the function that brings us the most pleasure will get our attention.

Think about the neurons that connect different spots in the brain to each other like a telephone circuit and all of a sudden only the happy conversations are being plugged in. Since humans have over 200 billion of these neuron connections, they are organized into pathways, like rivers of neuron charges as described in principle 1, they are interwoven and integrated. The more strength they have, the more power they have and they are very hard to redirect.

When a neuron is not used, it reconnects to something that will use it. It does not die from disuse; it reconfigures itself and attaches to the highest bidder, which again is a pleasure principle. In this case the elements that have the highest stimulation (drugs) will usually be the winners. If these forces begin to govern the whole brain, then the individual loses control and choice. What happens is that big holes, as seen in brain scans, start to appear in the brain, which limits its thinking capacity, especially in what motivates it. These are sometimes "holes" that lack brain tissue, but they can be holes of non-activity as well and may be close to dormant.

A metaphor scenario could help in understanding the process. Assume that a person has a diseased brain and looking for a purse that probably has 200 dollars in it. The person's mother's purse is unattended and the 200 dollars it has is going to pay the rent. In the person's mind that 200 dollars would go a long way in paying for his or her next high, and right now that person is desperate. In fact, that individual really thinks he or she is going to die if they don't get it.

The brain has already made that choice, regardless of how much that person may love their mother, regardless of how they know that she could lose her home, regardless of how much they know they are going to hurt her and disappoint her, that money is a survival level and the brain goes into survival mode. The moral fibers are gone or they are out of commission and no other thought can be entered into a decision. A person that has a mental disease like a psychopathic criminal in which there is no empathy or even second thoughts, but the psychopathology is based on neurological shift, not character logical flaws. That purse is a symbol of life by the brain's cognitive abilities and the brain's logical system justifies stealing it. To the addicted brain, this amounts to a life-threatening situation and its reflexes are fixed.

The interesting aspect as a neuro-psychologist is the direct association of the nucleus accumbens to the forebrain and how the immediacy of gratification is automatically rewired to the deeper regions of the amygdala. The forebrain lobe is associated with organizing our world and planning for the execution of our demands in order to assure our survival and pleasure. This is the part of the brain that is usually significantly dysfunctional in concentration functions, such as with attention deficit disorder. However, in this case more than normal demands are placed in priority of pleasure behaviors to be guided to the drug and alcohol cues in the brain.

The model of using the pleasure centers as the precise centers that govern the brain and related functions is a bit simplistic because the process starts throughout the neurological system, but it gives the model credibility in understanding the damaging forces in a person's motivations. The brain acts as an organizing and integrated system, so as the substances that stimulate the brain lead to toxicity and inflammation, the person's mind goes further into confusion and misdirection.

Add to this the intense memories associated with the drugs in the emotional centers of the amygdala and there is a constant looping, especially every time emotions arise by association. The use of drugs becomes hardwired to the brain and all motivations become geared to this objective. The trap is closed and choice becomes irrelevant to those already decided in the brain.

The next phase is the downgrading and destructive impact of the drugs themselves on the brain as the inflammation decays the inner structure of the mind. Judgment is lost, a life run by values loses its potentials and death in the organs adds to the disintegration of the body.

Miller and Rollnick (2002) reported on an interesting experiment in which they evaluated addicted subjects in an immediacy attention task. It is a very fancy piece of equipment to describe, but let us suffice to say that each subject had a split second to see a neutral object on the screen of a computer paired with two words, a word related to a drug or alcohol and a neutral word. The results indicated that the addicted people would automatically see the drug-associated word first in such a short time it was obvious that the person could not control the brain demand to attend to it. The reason for reporting this study is to validate the instinctive response the addictive brain has in focusing on drugs without any inhibition. The disease takes over all immediate reactions to any stimulation and places some form of addictive quality to it. It is like a person starving and with everything you mention, he thinks of food.

The results of having a brain rewire itself only toward pleasures will have the following consequences:

• Involuntary actions taken to gain more drugs for pleasures. These activities will produce a human with no remorse other than desperation for ways to get more drugs.

- No judgment for action other than the means necessary to acquire drugs and use.
- Subhuman priority system for desired actions limited to drugs and other stimulants.
- Multiple states of consciousness limited to three states: without drugs, with drugs, and unconscious.
- Build-up of toxicity in the body, which will create limitation and disease in the liver and other elimination organs (kidneys, lungs, and digestive track).
- Blockages of clearing channels for other medications and drugs such that side effects can be very confusing and even reversals of expected results, making treatment of emotional and mental symptoms problematic.

PSYCHOLOGICAL ADDICTIONS BECOME PHYSICAL ADDICTIONS

Drugs and alcohol addiction has a definite biological model for determining a basic qualification as a physical disease. There are concrete brain structures that become dysfunctional in brain maps and toxicity buildup creates tangible laboratory tests that would qualify a person to be physically sick and out of control.

What about food addiction, gambling addiction, or sex addiction? The question arises: could a person stop food obsession, gambling dependency, and sex/porno fixation if you held a gun to his or her head if he or she were to continue their behaviors? The answers would likely be yes, at least until they felt depressed or anxious again.

As the nucleus accumbens discover certain foods, gambling against big odds, or sexually arousing images, the brain operates similarly to drugs in that all of the connections for pleasures start creating a massive focus on these outlets. What is called the brain dynamics are "pathological gambling," "food obsession," "hyperactive sexual arousal," or some other psychological description without physical determinism. What is happening to the brain is basically similar in that a person's quality of life suffers from the brain imbalance in favor of these specific pleasures, but there is no way to demonstrate a physical disease category, although it can be treated similarly.

PROGRESSION OF THE DISEASE

The brain is our primary source of identification and provides the executive functions required to live a normal life. Drug and alcohol dependency is a major disease that is as vicious as a tumor and probably disrupts more functions overall.

These are a few of the functions that intertwine with every critical part of our lives:

- Judgment about priorities and organization of every part of our lives, including our own safety (driving, nutritional requirements, etc.)
- Moods of happiness and appropriate sadness are completely distorted and do not serve the person for motivations in insight or in behavior and attitude changes as a part of acquiring wisdom.
- Destroys trust and reliability by inconsistent priorities and loss of memory.
- Loss of memory can lead to a form of dementia.
- Value system destruction in all phases of life so that the only values are drugs and alcohol.
- Disruption of consciousness in critical times, which is similar to temporary amnesia, blackouts, loss of evaluation recall which relates to lack of memory before blackouts and function in responsible positions.
- Lack of overall functioning that is caused by decay of physical strength and body integrity through vitamin loss.

THE PROMISE OF THE BRAIN PLASTICITY MODEL

Because the brain can mobilize itself to maximize drug usage, it can also be mobilized toward health goals. A stroke victim who cannot speak due to a brain injury can be taught to use another part of the brain as a backup system and thus can relearn to speak again. An automobile accident crippled Frank from walking again due to a massive head injury, but through tremendous effort and retraining he taught his brain to use his legs in new ways and he now gets anywhere he wants. The same is true for the damage of brain toxicity and addiction. People prove it every day in terms of rewiring their brains.

Due to modern technology humans can now use strategic processes to rewire our emotional as well as our physical modes toward successful rehabilitation.

Coaching Principle

As part of any coaching career, the use of this principle to alter the brain patterns is truly what makes super star athletes. The formalization of non-addictive brain patterns follows the same steps. In order to lay down constructive tracks, there's a system that all great coaches utilize when developing fundamental skills in their team members. The three steps of brain pattern development are basic to all new or renewed strengthening patterns:

1. Demonstrate and create a visual image of the desired skill
2. Practice, practice, practice good behavioral skills
3. Celebrate success with positive feedback (Then repeat steps 1, 2, and 3.)

The implementation of this type of imagery has been used successfully in helping alcohol addicts as described earlier. To repeat, the patients imagine situations when they were more apt to abuse alcohol, such as being frustrated with authority, interpersonal conflicts, and periods of low self-esteem. The client would be asked to be specific to each potentially vulnerable situation—imagine what constructive steps they might take that would help foster a positive outcome. They were asked to do this mental exercise for no less than three scenarios.

Next, these individuals verbally walked through their imagined scenarios with their peer group; and it was the other group members' responsibility to ensure that no details—no matter how small—were left out so that every variable would be satisfied. For example, if a person imagined the act of calling a sponsor, he or she would be asked what their phone number is, the person's name, a backup person in the case their first choice is unavailable, what phone they would use, whose phone they would use if they didn't have access to first choice, what would be said, what the response would be, and so on. The individual would continue to retell the scenario until all details were rehearsed and complete clarity was achieved.

At the conclusion of each session, everyone in the group would write down their own three options in response to the scenarios and commit those plans to memory. This approach was a success with over 90 percent of the participants in the recovery process.

Clearly, the principle of brain plasticity has profound implications for effectively dealing with problems or potential issues. I call this process: *Making a Plan*. It may sound simple, but that's the point. Clients need clear simple plans to better handle chaos and unexpected situations.

Disrupting Behaviors

There are three processes that are basic, although nonetheless revolutionary, to all brain plasticity. The first is the process of dispersion or disruption, which must take place in our nerve patterns prior to assimilating new information. As you now know, it's exceedingly difficult to break habits neurologically or behaviorally merely by announcing a desire to do so. Smokers will attest to the experience of consistently meeting failure when attempting to break the smoking habit. Similarly, it's difficult to stop overreacting to your child when in conflict, or to stop obsessively worrying about your children when you've had so many reinforcing years of practice.

A process used for disrupting brain activity is called "altered states of consciousness" practice, where your conscious awareness of reality is deviated subjectively or psychologically. The most comprehensive (and complicated) definition is a pattern of physiological and subjective responses (cortical and autonomic), which shift with changes in imagery, ideation, and fantasies. These disruptions are generally anticipated and embraced in an effort to find preferable thinking habits. Another very powerful stimulation is rhythmic stimulation, such as music and drumming. The brain is sensitive to external rhythmic vibrations of any kind, and as humans will learn, the frequencies of the brain can be driven with such intention. This is the stuff of neurological training and finding the personal sonic stimulation that works best for your brain can be extraordinarily powerful.

Nutritional Power

For many years, diet in conjunction with other aspects such as exercise has had an important impact in shaping cognitive ability and brain evolution. In fact, there is a direct relationship between access to food and human brain size. Since brain development is a complex interactive process in which early disruptive events can have long-lasting effects on later functional adaptation, nutrition humans consume plays an essential role. Research has provided evidence for the influence of dietary factors on specific molecular systems and mechanisms that maintain mental function. The brain processes that are affected by diet are neurotransmitter pathways, synaptic transmission, membrane fluidity, and signal transduction pathways.

Several weeks ago there was a patient with symptoms of brain seizures that had a relationship to early brain trauma and while consulting with some colleagues from a center that specialized in seizures they said something that startled us. They recommended a number of specialized tests that had special relevance, but they said that they treated their patients with nutritional therapy as a priority. It was suspected that some customized regiment and prepared foods, but they simply replied that it was a "ketogenic diet," consisting of a basic high protein, high good fat diet with low carbs, and very low sugar content. It has been supported that a diet rich in omega 3 fatty acids, which are normal constituents of cell membranes and essential for brain function, support these cognitive processes and maintain synaptic function and plasticity and protect neurons from death. Food sources that have high omega 3 fatty acids are fish (salmon), flax seeds, krill, chia, kiwi fruit, butternuts, and walnuts. Fish oil supplements have been linked with improved cognitive function scores (Uauy, R., and Dangour, A. D. 2006). When clients arrive at Origins Recovery Center, they are given fish oil supplements daily to assist with brain detoxification and getting their brain back cognitively at a faster rate. In a research study, it was shown that an omega-3 fatty acid enriched diet can provide protection against reduced plasticity and impaired learning ability after a traumatic brain injury (Wu, Aiguo, Zhe Ying, and Fernando Gomez-Pinilla 2004).

In contrary, a diet that is high in saturated fats and has a deficiency of omega-3 fatty acids have been coupled with a higher risk of several mental health disorders and neurological dysfunction (Gómez-Pinilla 2008). In a particular study, a water-maze performance of mice fed a saturated-fat diet showed less complex patterns of dendritic branching. This demonstrates that one's diet, especially in the stages of detoxification of the brain for addicts, is critical to be mindful of. A diet high in saturated fat could lead to irreversible damage (Haast, and Kiliaan 2014). The most prominent example of a dietary treatment is the high fat, low carbohydrate ketogenic diet used in patients with epilepsy (Stafstrom, and Rho 2012). The ketogenic diet (refer to appendix B for a full printable list) relies on a fundamental change in the brain's metabolism from that of a glucose-based energy substrate to a ketone-based substrate. In other words, this diet forces the body to burn fats rather than carbohydrates. In a research study, twenty-three adults with mild cognitive impairment were given a high carbohydrate or low carbohydrate diet. After a six week intervention period, it was observed that there was improved verbal memory performance for the low carbohydrate adults in which the ketone levels were positively correlated with memory performance (Krikorian, Shidler, Dangelo, Couch, Benoit, and Clegg 2012). In working with addicts and alcoholics, this diet will contribute to improved plasticity while obtaining sobriety.

With some literature review and discussion, it makes good sense that the brain's best food for rehabilitation is fats, but if sugar is the main element, it will not facilitate healing. Seizure activity is not discussed here, instead focusing on brain healing from inflammation and toxic exposure is the goal. The fact that this food group is successful 90 percent of the time for the severe brain damage that produces seizures is very significant.

Many foods have been implicated in increasing learning curves, and I have found this approach to have high impact, whether it is for better control or actual growth factor influence. High protein (as in eggs and meat), Omega 3 and 6 (as in fish) and some complex carbohydrates have some pretty meaningful impact in this regard. This ketogenic food diary can be found in appendix B.

Physical Exercise for the Brain

The pursuit of physical activity has been present since the existence of mankind. In the earliest days, physical activity was a need for survival and was activated through hunting and gathering. Fast forward to today and physical fitness is a way to stay fit and be healthy and is even considered a sport. Physical exercise has been accomplished for many reasons and today scientists know through evidence that exercise builds brain health in a phenomenal way.

Human and animal studies conclude that exercise targets many aspects of brain function and has broad effects on overall brain health and brain plasticity. Benefits of exercise have been best defined for learning, memory, protection of neurogenesis (birth of new nerve cells), alleviation of depression, and neurotransmission. Exercise excites brain regions that are involved in memory function to release a chemical called brain–derived neurotrophic factor (BDNF). BDNF rewires memory circuits and stimulates neurogenesis. This increases resistance to brain insult and improves learning and mental performance (Cotman and Berchtold 2002). Exercise increases synaptic plasticity by directly affecting synaptic structure and potentiating synaptic strengths and by strengthening underlying systems that support plasticity including metabolism and vascular function. In addition, exercise reduces peripheral risk factors such as diabetes, hypertension, and cardiovascular disease, which converge to cause brain dysfunction and neurodegeneration (Cotman, Berchtold, and Christie 2007).

Studies have also shown that certain neurotransmitters can be affected by exercise. The systems that are affected by exercise are the central dopaminergic, noradrenergic, and serotonin systems. Because physical exercise affects dopamine, noradrenaline, and serotonin, it has been reported to reduce depression and anxiety and improve coping skills (Chaouloff 1989). In particular, running is a rewarding anti-depressant. In an animal model of depression, increasing neurogenesis with a low intensity or moderate running exercise in the hippocampus is beneficial as an anti-depressant (Brené, Bjørnebekk, Åberg, Mathé, Olson, and Werme 2007). With sustained physical activity, such as running, an increase in neurotropic levels occurs with prolonged low intensity exercise while higher intensity exercise in a rat model of brain injury elevates the stress hormone, corticosterone (Ploughman 2008). This goes to show that exercise does not have to be strenuous in order to have cognitive rewards. Since exercise has been shown to increase neurocognitive function, it is encouraged for patients that are undergoing a rehabilitation process aiding the brain to heal from the impact of their drug of choice.

Meditation and Neuroplasticity

Meditation refers to a broad variety of practices, ranging from techniques designed to promote relaxation to exercises performed with a purpose of reaching higher goals such as a sense of well-being in the world (Davidson, and Lutz 2008). Meditation is a family of complex emotional and attentional regulatory practices that can be classified into two

main styles: focused attention (FA) and open monitoring (OM) meditation. These two practices involve different attentional, cognitive monitoring or awareness processes (Manna et al. 2010). The two common styles
of meditation are often combined either in a single meditation session or
over the course of the meditator's practice.

Investigators of neuroplasticity demonstrate that the adult brain can
continue to form novel neural connections and grow new neurons in
response to learning or training even into old age (Garland and Howard
2009). When the framework of neuroplasticity is applied to meditation, it
is suggested that the mental training of meditation is no different than
other forms of skill acquisition that can induce plastic changes in the
brain (Davidson and Lutz 2008). Recent studies have found evidence of
functional and structural changes in the brain following meditation practice, indicating that meditation harnesses the brain's inherent ability to
change in response to experience (Skeide 2010).

The amount of time an individual spends practicing meditation is
associated with activity and connectivity changes in the brain that are
shown even during the resting, non-meditative state. This means that
brain networks trained during meditation can be rewired to have lasting
changes that extend to mental experiences (Hasenkamp and Barsalou
2012). In a particular study, scans of Buddhist monks' brains and novice
volunteer meditators were compared during meditation. There was a
remarkable difference between the experienced monks' and the novices'
brain. Although the novice meditators had a slight increase in high frequency brain activity called gamma waves, the monks showed a dramat-
ic increase in these gamma waves that underlie higher mental activity
such as consciousness. This suggests that with meditative mental training, the brain can indeed be brought to a higher level of consciousness
(Begley 2004). In addition, meditation practices have been importantly
associated with reorganization of activity patterns in the pre-frontal cortex, the site of positive emotions such as happiness (Manna et al. 2010).
Furthermore, using magnetic resonance imaging, it has been observed
that there is higher gray matter density in the lower brain stem regions of
experienced meditators versus people who did not meditate at all (Vestergaard-Poulsen, van Beek, Skewes, Bjarkam, Stubberup, Bertelsen, and
Roepstorff 2009). Higher gray matter in this region correlates with a
heightened control over cardiovascular and respiratory systems. This allows meditators to control heart and respiration rhythms, as well as having an influence over immune systems, alertness, and sleep quality. Meditation can increase quality of life and most importantly opens up the
reality that the human brain can and will be altered intentionally in the
same way humans alter their muscles.

Bio and Neuro Feedback

According to the International Society for Neurofeedback and Research (ISNR), bio/neuro feedback is a process that enables an individual to learn how to change physiological activity for the purposes of improving health and performance. Precise instruments measure physiological activity such as brainwaves, heart function, breathing, muscle activity, and skin temperature. These types of instruments rapidly and accurately give "feedback" information to the user. The presentation of this information, often in conjunction with changes in thinking, emotions, and behavior, supports desired physiological changes. Over time, these changes can endure without continued use of an instrument. Bio and neuro feedback allows the person a greater awareness of physiological functions and allows them to control their breathing and thoughts to control different aspects of their activity at will. Feedback exercise can affect reaction time, attention, general cognition, memory, and several other measures of mental function (Carmeli 2014).

Neuroplasticity is possible due to two main neurophysiological processes: neurogenesis and synaptogenesis. One of the most effective tools in neuroplasticity is the use of bio and neuro feedback. In order for new synapses and pathways to be formed and developed, neurons must be stimulated; bio/neuro feedback can activate this growth. The devices used offers external and internal feedback training in an interactive, motivated, and safe way to explore and relearn motor skills and cognitive capacities (Carmeli 2014). After retraining adults with mild traumatic brain injuries and ADHD using twenty biofeedback treatment sessions, results found a significant improvement on full scale attention and full scale response accuracy of a continuous performance task in the traumatic brain injury and ADHD groups compared to the control group (Tinius and Tinius 2000).

In Heart Rate Variability (HRV) biofeedback, individuals can learn to increase the amplitude of their heart rate variable, the variation in the time interval between heart beats, oscillations by breathing at specific rates (Breach 2012). HRV biofeedback increases specific bands of brain activity as measured by an EEG. During biofeedback relaxation in which subjects learn to decrease sympathetic arousal, there is enhanced anterior cingulate activity, an area of the brain associated with emotion. This data implicate the anterior cingulate cortex in the intentional modulation of bodily arousal and suggests how cognitive states are integrated with bodily responses (Critchley, Melmed, Featherstone, Mathias, and Dolan 2001). HRV biofeedback has been found to be effective at significantly reducing depression symptoms (Breach 2012). Functional imaging experiments have implicated specific brain areas in the generation and feedback representation of autonomic arousal. These regions include those associated with emotion and attention (Critchley, Melmed, Featherstone, Mathias, and Dolan 2001). In addition, heart rate variability bio-feedback stimulates barorelex response, the body's homeostatic mechanism which helps to maintain blood pressure at nearly constant levels, and is associated with cumulative barorelex gain, thought to be reflective of neuroplasticity (Sigafus 2013).

Biofeedback has been helpful in a rehabilitation setting for various reasons. Since maximal control over HRV can be obtained in most people after just four training sessions (Sutarto, Wahab, and Zin 2010), it does not take long for the client or patient to feel their arousal state shift. In a particular study, 121 volunteers undergoing an inpatient substance abuse program were randomly assigned to forty to fifty sessions of biofeedback or a control group. While the biofeedback group accomplished their training, the control group would get extra time in the rehabilitation setting. Overall, the experimental subjects that were given biofeedback sessions remained in treatment longer than the control group. Furthermore, twelve months after the study, the biofeedback group had a 77 percent rate of sobriety versus the control group having only a 44 percent rate of sobriety. Biofeedback can enhance treatment retention, variable of attention, and abstinence rates one year following treatment (Scott, Kaiser, Othmer, and Sideroff 2005). For bio and neuro feedback to be most effective and beneficial it should include the following features: motivation, challenge point framework, associative function, guidance, and assurance of safety (Carmeli 2014).

Finding Our Internal Compass

It is unsettling to note that people plan their whole lives according to the pleasure principle, yet they continue to neglect this principle repeatedly and largely because they lose faith that life can be joyful. Life starts with the rhythms of our mothers' hearts and becoming attuned to our own. Each of our cells has their combined rhythms and the perception of the world is noted by the different modes of sensory cell combinations. Our world has its different seasons and days and night variations. How could people not know that our lives are ruled by the different seasonal changes? Patience and practicing the rules of a healthy life must be taught to our clients in order for them to mature as wise and respectful members of society during the recovery process.

When a client gets admitted into a treatment center for addiction, their internal compass is set on the character of the ego, based on selfish needs and wants. Part of the process of recovery is working the Twelve Steps of AA and allowing the internal healer to take over in order to let go of ego completely. Of course, this could be a difficult process since the brain has been wired on the pleasure principle. In Step Two of the Twelve Steps of AA, the addict must find a power greater than themselves in order to be restored to sanity. This opens the addict's eyes to a different path other than the motivation of pleasure from the drug or alcohol. One of the tools used in neuroplasticity is the sensory deprivation chamber, a device that allows the mind to be deprived of all external stimuli. Through my experience, a large number of addicts that have had an experience in the sensory deprivation chamber come to a spiritual almost enlightened place. Susan was a client that had rejected the notion of any power greater than herself and found herself angry at the concept of any greater being. She struggled with alcoholism after her son was brutally and mysteriously killed while he was away at college. She questioned why there would be a God that would take away her only child, her baby boy who had brought so much joy into her life. She stepped into the sensory deprivation chamber thinking, "I am just going to lay in here in darkness experiencing absolutely nothing, what's the point?" She was quite vocal about her disbelief but curiosity always won her over and allowed her to step inside. After around forty-five minutes, Susan allowed me to open the hood of the sensory deprivation chamber. There was Susan full of tears and then she exclaimed, "I saw her!" After some calming and explanation, it was revealed that Susan had a visit from her deceased mother. Her mother told her there was a God who was taking care of her and that her son was at peace. From this day on, Susan held a new perspective on the power of spirit which allowed her to work Step Two and hold the belief there was a power greater than self that could (and did) restore her to sanity. Susan recently celebrated one year of sobriety and every time Origins Recovery Center hears from Susan, she still mentions the spiritual experience that was instrumental to her process.

Part of the recovery progression is having the addict make amends to people that they have wronged during their active addiction (Step Nine in AA). There is a definite structure on how this amends process is carried out and it can lead to intense social or performance anxiety. There can also be tough situations brought forth that take a tremendous amount of courage to face. Scott, a middle aged man from Ohio, created a wide path of destruction for himself during his active addiction. Scott would get into the habit of stealing and indeed got away with it for a while. He began to experience extreme guilt and shame when having to confront close friends and family that he stole from. Scott worked an intense stress management program in the Psychoneuroplasticity Center and by the end of the program he learned a diaphragmatic breathing technique that could help him cope with social anxiety. Through the anxiety management program, Scott learned the principles of biofeedback and most importantly how to develop a breathing pattern for increased relaxation in order to handle situations such as making amends. In fact, Scott learned his anxiety-based tendencies so well that he recognized what is called stress signals—cues that the body gives and tells the person they are undergoing a stressful situation. Stress signals, such as irritability, nail biting, pain, or tension headaches, informed Scott when his stress level would increase and provided a cue to use his coping strategies such as the diaphragmatic breathing or repeating a mantra. Scott never imagined being able to face the people he disappointed and make amends for his wrong doings but when he made a visit back home to Ohio he developed the strength to accomplish just this. The fear, the anxiety, and the anger he held toward himself melted away as he practiced the coping skills he learned.

Allison grew up in a home with rigid religious practices. She went to a Catholic school and attended Sunday school regularly. While sitting in church most rituals felt very robotic for her. She always noticed that she would day dream in church service and never felt any different after leaving mass. Allison never understood the elation or refreshing feeling others would speak about after church. She knew there was a higher power, but never fully understood him the way they described him in church. As she got older, she started to rebel against the strict standards her family held for her and eventually fell into drugs and alcohol. This cycle became out of control and her family and friends, knew it so they called an intervention. Since Allison cared about her family and really had no choice, she admitted herself into treatment. While in treatment, Allison confided that she did not know how to get in contact with her higher power, which she now called the "power of the universe." As Allison progressed through the AA program and came to Step Eleven, she learned that through constant prayer and meditation she could improve her conscious contact with the power of the universe. Allison learned different avenues and ways she could come into contact with her god at the PNP center. Allison started with the simple concept of quieting and using her breath to become close to spirit. Allison had always thought that breathing was just the simple movement of bringing air in and out of her body but soon came to find out that the way she breathed affected the state of mind she was in. She found out that breathing deeply and slowly created a peaceful state in her mind, heart, and soul. As she practiced her breathing technique opened up a new world. With each meditation, Allison was able to gain stepping stones that furthered her spiritual aspect of life. Eventually, Allison came to find out that drumming was the most powerful way for her to experience her spirituality fully. Allison would listen to the beat of the drum and get connected to the intrinsic rhythm of the energy of the world. Allison finally found out what that refreshing feeling felt like and realized that she just needed to find her own path to knowing the god of her own understanding.

Each of these clients opened up a portal to their internal compass by having the courage to take hold of their recovery process. They found many gifts along the way but with the gifts come with struggles or barriers that must be faced in order to obtain the greatest gift of all- a fruitful and meaningful life.

Part II

Barriers to Recovery

The successful path to recovery is not usually a straight line; there is a reason for an 80 percent probability of a relapse. Not only is the brain damaged after substance abuse, but the family structure around a person's life is often in shambles, never to be the same again, and the person has to rebuild a lifetime of trust in their community as well as in themselves. The other barriers to recovery are likely to have been set even before the abuse started and begin to raise their ugly heads when the climb to sobriety and sanity begins.

The ugliest ones are the worst self-descriptions the patients describe when they call upon the strengths to transcend the mountain of recovery that builds upon self-esteem and competence. These are the underlying assaults their parents made upon their characters when they undermined the patient's self-worth. Perhaps the most insidious are the fears and anxieties that mount within their attempts to rise above their wars and demons, or the ongoing rage they wage upon themselves. Described in the following chapters are paths through and around their barriers that can be accomplished at the brain level where a level playing field with the soul can be prepared.

FIVE

Anxiety Barriers of Confusion and Fear

Divan's history was not rare among addiction sufferers. He could not remember a day he was not anxious about his life. His mother was an alcoholic who never took time to be a nurturing mother. Either she was drunk or sick from being drunk. He did not worry so much about her drinking episodes, even though he dreaded them, especially when she would tell him "secrets" he did not want to hear, like the ones of her lovers who did her wrong or the confusion in her mind as to which man was his real father. He was more worried that she would die and all of his world would turn to nothing, no roots and no family, no expectations for his life, no rhythm to feel life as an even flow, just a series of barriers and challenges.

Divan had one advantage in life—he was smart. His teachers liked him, in spite of the worn-out clothes he wore. He loved school because he felt he had a level playing field with the other kids, and competition usually gave him a step up on the others. He was also big for his age with a very handsome face. He used all of his skills and advantages anytime he could to win the race for highest grades.

One year a young teacher sought Divan out as a young scholar and took him on as his assistant. Unfortunately, this young teacher taught him things he didn't need to know for success. He was molested all that year with promises of "A"s regardless of performances for sexual secrecy and threatened him with dismissal if the secrets saw light.

Divan felt guilty and worried that his educational career would end with the slightest hint of lack of loyalty. His social relationships became distant as he became more paranoid. He became more obsessive about his grades and studied every hour he could, partly because of his need to

63

get financial support for college through scholarships and partly to blank his mind from his molestation.

Divan won his scholarship to a high-level university and majored in political science with the mission of helping other children just like him. But the road through college was more labile for emotional disaster than high school. He was involved in three more sexual relationships with teachers, but he was not as stressed as the earlier one because he was doing what he had to do to get his degree, and if that was his price, he would sell his soul to get through.

Divan's recipe for success followed him into law school except the sexual issues, probably because the professors had no interest in such activities and the atmosphere was much different than college. Although the molestations in the past created enormous stress on him, he did assume that a big reason for his success was his sexual nature and not his intelligence, making law school a major assault on what he regarded as tools to defeat the system.

The program was very competitive and Divan's study habits could have kept the pace, but his anxiety proved to be his worst enemy. He could concentrate long enough to grasp the concepts being taught, but his memory didn't appear to last ten minutes. He was on academic probation his first semester and his future was very dismal. He was in a constant state of panic and found a new way to deal with his issues—drugs.

The rest of the story is predictable. He found a physician who would diagnose him as ADHD and prescribed him a continuous fountain of Adderall, a stimulant, which helped him concentrate. He ate it like candy, which only made him more anxious and fearful, even paranoid. He had constant headaches and his blood pressure soared. He felt that he was going to go psychotic. Although he was never a drinker in college, because he was so ambitious, now alcohol was his vacation away from school and where he found a sense of peace. He finally felt normal.

He started drinking on the weekends when school demands were not crushing down on him, but soon the peace became more important than classes, and the weekends started growing from Thursday to Tuesday, and quickly became a seven-day weekend. In spite of the fact that he knew he would be terminated from law school at the end of the semester, he continued to receive his student loans to live on, so he made the best of it. For the first time he could remember he felt like a normal person, although he didn't act normally. He spent the night in jail several times for public intoxication and drained every penny in his bank account on partying. When his academic career came to an end, he was homeless, sleeping under a bridge.

DIVAN TAKES CONTROL

During those periods when the money he begged for ran out or jail times when he reached a level of sobriety of rational thought, he would make himself promises to rise above his mental obsession with "feeling normal" and restart his life. He finally ended up in detox and then a 30-day program where he was monitored enough to start making some goals. He wanted to be "in control" of his life again.

His motivation was good and he made it a competition to get through the Twelve Steps in record time without internalizing, obviously missing the whole concept of recovery. However, he did stay sober for two weeks before he relapsed. He explained, "the pain of being sober is too much and too boring." His life style was a challenge to deal with the barriers to peace. Divan's barriers could be confined to what is defined as Anxiety I category.

ANXIETY DEFINED

Anxiety is defined in the *Diagnostic and Statistical Manual of Mental Disorders* (American Psychiatric Association [Ed.]. 2000) as a state of consciousness in which a person worries excessively without having the ability to control it. Restlessness, being easily fatigued, difficulty breathing, concentrating, irritability, muscle tension, and disturbed sleep patterns often accompany this state and can be the precursor to using sedative drugs and alcohol. Anxiety can also be the basis for other syndromes, such as obsessive-compulsive disorders, over-focus on health issues (hypochondriasis), and phobias.

Anxiety is also considered to be a normal human condition because 70 percent of adults say they experience it on a daily basis, and 30 percent report their anxiety levels are constant. Anxiety is based on fear, and this psychological state is instinctual to our survival, and socialization. Not all anxiety is considered destructive. Many people successfully use anxiety as a form of motivation to achieve higher goals, that is, they look forward to experiencing a profound sense of relief once they've accomplished their goal. For example, they may set a goal that is rather irrelevant to life, such as driving home after work in record time compared to previous times. It may excite a person to push limits and stay within the law, but they may also show some frustration if they make some wrong choices and lose time. The individual may have also used a self-inflicted goal for making grades in school or writing a paper. Anxiety can serve an individual as a push for achievement—or, it can seriously get in the way.

Anxiety has been associated with many psychological diagnoses. It can be the underlying denominator of post-traumatic stress disorder (PTSD), panic, and multiple personality. Anxiety can also trigger various personality disorders, such as borderline personality disorder and dependency disorders. Particularly disconcerting, the anxiety clusters can trigger borderline personality disorders to become dangerous and has resulted in violent crimes, domestic abuse, homicide, and suicide. While this disorder has a benign-sounding name, it's anything but.

Anxiety doesn't have to become a threat to esteem, progress toward a goal, or to anyone else for that matter. The objective is to get past the anxiety brain trap. It may be helpful to imagine what's going on in the anxiety-filled brain: Fear and stress trigger the brain into an anxiety frustration, which triggers chaos that the brain tries to resolve but can't. Instead, the fears and frustrations just linger there, endlessly spinning, with surges of raw shocks. This means the person gets into trouble by remaining in a state of chronic anxiety. There doesn't have to be any obvious external sources of stress in life for the brain to be on "spin." Anxiety brain patterns can be generated by merely worrying or stewing about what might have happened in the past, or what might happen in the future. Fear begets fear.

THE ANXIETY BRAIN PATTERN

In the same way that anxiety triggers the brain circuitry to get stuck on a fear and stress treadmill, rage (and violence) triggers immediacy to action without rational processing. When a person's brain is smoldering with hot high beta waves, it only takes a tiny spark of heightened arousal (like misplacing a pencil, or seeing someone they dislike) to set a person off into an illogical, full-blown rage.

This counterproductive brain pattern can get so tightly locked; it becomes very difficult for the person to justify his behavior to him- or herself (or to anyone else). Plus, the person becomes unable to gain control or glean any insight as to why they are reacting this way—which of course increases their level of agitation (and everyone else's, too). As long as the brain storm is dictating how one thinks, all of the insight, education, and psychotherapy in the world will only get a person so far. To truly get off the treadmill, one needs to unlock the brain door. But first, the person must see the door. And that's the first step.

When using a QEEG brain *map*, patterns are very easy to see. Figure 5.1 A is a frontal lobe brain wave pattern. Notice how it is raging with high and electrical beta output. This is called a high beta anxiety storm. Figure 5.1 B is what a low beta wave pattern looks like.

Electromagnetic Storm Brewing—In Progress

Figure 5.2 illustrates what a brain in a chaotic state looks like, when measured as electromagnetic frequencies. This person's brain is not func-

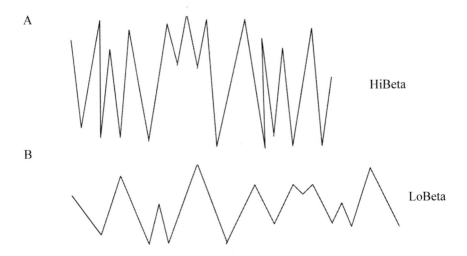

Figure 5.1. Differential Beta Frequencies

tioning at optimal levels. And the longer and more stress this brain has to endure, the more the pathways will continue and build.

BAUD Entrainment in Disrupting Anxiety Pathways

When psychoneuroplasticity methods were first conceived for anxiety, the goal was attempts to help chronic pain patients in an intensive rehabilitation program. A drumming rhythm (theta range) by a shaman practitioner was taught that was later shown to entrain brain frequencies to slow down to theta level functions. This rhythmic sound application led to an invention of a sonic device called the BAUD (BioAcoustical Utilization Device), which does the same thing only the rhythms can be altered to any frequency desired and the entrainment can result in retraining of anxiety pathways.

The device has been specifically used for anxiety patterns in the PNP Center, and although it is not necessary, the actual patterns of the person's EEG brain pattern are measured to justify the conclusions that the anxiety patterns disappear.

Method: The patient is asked, "How high is your anxiety on a scale from 1 (low anxiety) to 10 (very high anxiety) for a pre-measure. The BAUD has four control knobs, two on top and two on the bottom. The lower two are volume controls, one for each ear. The top right knob controls the frequencies of both ears, and the instructions to the client is to gradually turn the frequencies to a point that he or she becomes relaxed. When that occurs, the instructions are to find a setting on the upper left knob that helps reduce the anxiety even more. When that

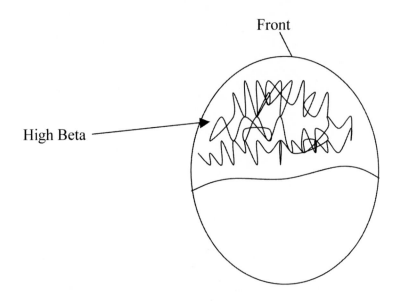

Figure 5.2. Associated Brain Map for Anxiety

occurs, have the patient find any tweaking of the sonic signals to maximize the feelings of relaxation. Then assess the feeling sense on the same
1-10 scale as used in the beginning.

Aaron started to use marijuana at the age of ten spurred on by his
older brother's banter and encouragement. Aaron's drug use spun out of
control to the point of unmanageability and came to a point where he
knew he needed help. When Aaron decided to come to treatment because
of his addiction, he allowed his body to come off all substances that he
had been using since a very young age. Aaron came to find out that he
was extremely anxious without his drugs and found that he had no coping skills to deal with any real-world situations. Aaron came into the first
PNP session with clammy, shaky hands and a frigid demeanor. At first,
Aaron was not a believer that the sonic stimulation device could help him
reduce anxiety at all, ever since he could remember when he was without
his drugs he would go into a "spin out state" of anxiety. After allowing
the sonic stimulation to take over the anxiety, Aaron immediately felt his
perception change and felt like he was able to "calm down and breathe."
The next day Aaron had a huge smile on his face and proclaimed that he
never knew he could get a handle on his anxiety monster.

Imagine the type of excitement Aaron found, a way of controlling the
anxiety of the brain in a matter of minutes. The smiles are common because at any time of the day, or night, the BAUD is available to redirect
the brain patterns without pills or even therapy. There are consistent

reports of school and work successes with the use of the BAUD, and this can be a central alternative to drugs and prevention of relapse.

Listen to the Music

The oldest way to stop the brain from getting stuck into an anxiety brain storm is to turn on some music. The tempo and melody of favorite songs can dial stress levels down to manageable emotions in about fifteen minutes. Some personal favorites are Mozart, Cher, and Simon and Garfunkel. What types of music will help a person relax is a personal choice. Whatever the musical preference, research clearly shows that self–selected relaxing music significantly reduces anxiety and nervous system arousal. The imagery of the neurons begin to join a chorus in the alpha zone can be visualized. Also, if an instrument is played in a way that one finds soothing, the research shows that is a great stress/anxiety reducer as well.

Move to Your Relaxation Beat

The body literally likes rhythmic, soothing movement. Yoga and Tai'Chi are particularly effective in getting motor neurons "hooked up" with feeling soothed. And of course, dancing is great. As a required part of therapy, anxious patients are encouraged to dance with a drumming CD, called "Life Rhythms," as part of their homework for twenty-two minutes per day. This requirement has also been especially effective for medical students who are so anxiety-filled that they start failing their classes, even when they totally understood the topics being evaluated. Without exception, they report that moving to the beat helps them to feel "different and better" and clearly not as fearful the first week; by the second week, they turn the corner and find new directions for their lives. Incidentally, this CD is a basic homemade recording of some continuous conga drums and a few other acoustical instruments, but unsophisticated as it is, it works. If the patient is so inclined, they can make their own CD. Otherwise, finding a rhythmic tune is a snap these days: Just search on-line or for the audio series at the mindbodyseries website (MindBodySeries).

Sing to the Brain

The power of music can get more complex. The experience has been that when brains are stimulated by rhythms at the beat of 60 bpm the frequencies of the cognitive gates appear to open and things are learned most easily. That is the reason children learn best through music, like the ABCs. This interest in rhythm continues to enable new concepts to be adopted to the mindset easier without resistance, especially with the other rhythms designed for problems such as marching rhythms with the thought that this type of rhythm is used by the military to bring individuals into a community unity, so it might be helpful for people who feel lonely and separated.

When these rhythms are integrated with lyrics in rap songs, some fascinating outcomes resulted. Dr. Susan Franks of the University of North Texas adopted the concept and she prepared three sets of lyrics to a nutritional program for sixth graders. This program was sponsored by Coca-Cola in its first year as a program to change children's eating behavior; it was called "Stomp for Life." The lyrics of the first song are in support of "Go Foods," the second is "No Foods" and the third is "Slow Foods." The "*go* foods" are healthy choices, the "*no* foods" are not healthy, and the "*slow* foods" are foods that should not be eaten every day. The children learned a short dance to each of the three sets of songs and beat out the rhythm with various forms of household appliances (toilet plungers, brooms, etc., or drum sticks).

The results have been astonishing (Franks 2011). The amazing thing is that these children actually liked the class and voluntarily requested to take it again. The second result is that these children have learned the contents and could recite the intended content; further, reports from the parents said that the children would start correcting them as to what food was best and would ask for the good foods instead. The astonishing results were that signs of diabetes (spots around the neck) reversed themselves for most of those children with those symptoms.

Lyrics were developed for drug issues, especially alcohol and set to rap backgrounds and played at a similar rhythm to the ones used in the Franks report. The results are yet to be analyzed from selecting that specific influences to the mindsets of those involved in the addiction program but all the patients know the lyrics by heart and enjoy singing the phrases with each other. With the words instilled in the brain, it was expected that just like the earlier findings the message of self-control will bind to the unconscious and prevent relapse.

Take Deep, Cleansing Breaths

There are over two thousand organs and hormones that can be affected positively or negatively in a matter of minutes by shifting your breathing patterns. When it comes to the brain, taking quick, shallow breaths usually signals the brain that a threat exists, which stimulates a stress response, and therefore destructive thinking patterns. Conversely, taking slow, deep breaths usually signals the brain that the coast is clear and all is well.

The best model to calm the storms is a technique referred to as the "circle breath." The name comes from the idea of keeping a steady exchange of air inhaling and exhaling, thereby creating a circle of airflow through the lungs. This is done in a relaxed manner utilizing imagery, such as inhaling while visualizing good nurturing air coming into the body and mind and then exhaling while thinking about releasing your inner toxins and unhealthy mental habits out into the ethers.

Until this technique is mastered, it may be beneficial to have someone coach an individual through this breathing pattern. It can be difficult (at first) to maintain concentration and focus while experiencing an anxiety stress storm. The suggestion is to listen to professionally prepared CDs of relaxing instructions, such as the Relaxation Breathing for Deep Peace or the Relaxation Focus version (MindBodySeries) by Dr. Frank Lawlis.

Catch the Breath "Wave"

The *emWave*™ (HeartMath LLC.2014) is a device that uses breathing patterns to regulate brain patterns through coordination with the heart rhythms, and has a computer than gives a personal breathing pace to coordinate with heart pace. The idea is that when a person has anxiety patterns, the brain is out of synch with the rest of the body. So, if the individual can learn to appropriately pace their breathing, he or she will also be doing the heart and the rest of the body a double service.

The rhythmic breathing not only tends to balance the relationship between the brain and heart, it also balances other systems within the body, especially the hormones. A centering effect happens when a person is regulating his or her breathing in step with the heart rate. More importantly, when the brain finds a peaceful pace within itself, the lightning neuro-storms cease. There is a sense of calm. After biofeedback training, patients usually report feeling as if they were floating or a sense of "feeling tingly" all over their body. It is amazing how much anxiety is lifted with using breath as the calming vehicle. Most importantly, the individual has learned a skill of breathing and controlling anxiety for the rest of their life.

Biofeedback and Aromas

One avenue to the brain pathway is the olfactory system. The fact that the olfactory system is the only one that connects directly to the brain instead of traveling to other areas of the brain is incredible. While other sensory processes travel along the thalamic route to the primary cortical region that processes the sensory information, the olfactory system travels directly to the forebrain. In order words, the effect of an aroma can be instantaneous and provoke a direct neurological and psychological effect on a person. When an aroma is smelled, there are 10 million olfactory cells, each of which has 350 different receptors in the nose that communicate with the olfactory cortex, amygdala, and hippocampus, which stores memories and emotions (Hawkes and Doty 2009). These receptors are each specialized to distinguish particular aromas. There are also researchers that believe that smelling essential oils stimulates parts of the brain that influence physical, emotional, and mental health. Aromas have been used for therapeutic purposes for nearly 6,000 years. Essential oils have been used for spiritual, therapeutic, and ritualistic purposes all over the world. The Chinese were the first to use aromatherapy with the use of incense to create balance and harmonic settings. The Egyptians used incense from aromatic woods to honor their gods with the belief that the smoke would rise into the heavens carrying their well wishes. In France, Dr. Jean Valnet used aromatherapy to treat illnesses, gangrene, and battle wounds. Jean Valnet wrote the book Practice of Aromatherapy (Valnet 2012), placing this practice on the map with an important piece of literature.

In a study by the department of nursing at Geochang Provincial College, the effects of the inhalation method using essential oils on blood pressure and stress responses of clients with essential hypertension were measured. The results found were the blood pressure, pulse, subjective stress, state anxiety, and serum cortisol levels among the three groups were significantly statistically different. This concludes that the inhalation method of using essential oils can be considered an effective nursing intervention that reduces psychological stress responses and serum cortisol levels, as well as the blood pressure of clients with essential hypertension (Hwang 2006). Taking the information above to augment biofeedback and allowing the client to be responsible for the outcome of their training. Heart rate variability biofeedback is a technique that is useful in reducing stress and depression. When biofeedback is coupled with aromatherapy, it was discovered that the self-report of the client brings a greater reduction of anxiety and an increased state of happiness. Since the olfactory system is primitive, even more primitive than drugs, this is a useful technique to use in the addiction setting. When a strong aroma is smelled by the client, there is an immediate disruption in the neurological connections that causes instantaneous change that goes past the cortex into the core brain areas. This supports Brain Plasticity Principle II, in the way that neurological bundles are changed by experience and in this case disruption. In our neuroplasticity sessions, the client will come in and choose from a wide variety of smells (from peppermint, eucalyptus, lavender to coconut and lime). The client dabs the essential oil on a pulse point and is instructed to smell the aroma when they achieve a deep state of relaxation or high coherence (indicated as a green light indicating high coherence with the EmWave biofeedback device). The client is instructed to follow the pacer on the biofeedback device with their abdominal breathing along with their choice of essential oil smell activating memories of relaxation. After a thirty minute period of biofeedback training, the client reports their relaxation level and state of being. For some time after the session, clients report that the simple whiff of the smell of their essential oil used during their biofeedback training brings them back into relaxation immediately. Not only does this technique bring the client a deeper state of relaxation, it also gets them more engaged in their abdominal breathing process which is crucial in many aspects of life and well-being.

Laughter

Laughter is also a good way to distract from fear-based anxiety. From years of extensive study in pain, the body is programmed to tolerate a maximum of pain. The real threat from chronic pain is that it is enduring—but keep in mind that one can battle this pain if the person can laugh at it, so that he or she can handle it for shorter periods. Biologically, there is nothing that can defeat a person, and the mental side has the major advantage of input. As an aside, even fear of death can be diminished (i.e., laughing in the face of death) if one can embrace the belief that life on the other side is wonderful thing. There are credible reports of people who've had near-death experiences who corroborate this belief.

Meditate in Action

Much research has been done in "mindfulness meditation," and it really helps formulate excellent prevention for anxiety (Miller, Fletcher, and Kabat-Zinn 1995). The main theme is to focus on the present only, neither the past nor future, just be where the mind is and what is present at the time. Notice the present smells, temperature on the skin, listen to the sounds, and so on. This form of meditation may sound too simple to work, but it's in fact a very powerful tool, and if practiced can evoke major transformation.

For those who were born with the work ethic that one has to be "productive" to be worthy will understand that it doesn't work that way if one doesn't understand how one can work in the present. What happens is that when you begin to look at the end result and only think of that as the goal, one places the brain thinking in two undesirable phases. The person places all value on the completion of the task and not on how well one is accomplishing the task. This is quantity instead of quality evaluation for the brain. This is the problem with many athletes. They think about the final score and winning instead of the special efforts at that instance of performance. They often forget the immediate gratification of the exchange one has against an opponent and the respect one gains for both individuals in the competition when one can live in the moment.

The principle of living in the present moment is that a person can focus on the here and now, making the best decisions at the time. One can begin to enjoy the immediate challenge. If a person only focuses attention on the future, he or she will miss a big part of life and lose huge amounts of pleasure. There is a wonderful story about a teenager that used to dig ditches for many utility companies and when he was told about focusing on each shovel full of dirt, time lost its power over him and he began to look forward to every task he faced. His brain was focused on what he was doing correctly, not on what he was lacking. If one thinks about the present moment it is the only time people are actually alive. Humans are not alive in the past nor do they know that they will be alive in the future, it is essential to hold the present moment as precious.

The gift of any opportunity is to embrace each and every second of the investment in it. Besides the huge cost of stress in thinking of us only in terms of producers, people let pass the greatest amount of time that they could enjoy. People are aging and miss most of their lives until it is too late. The only thing that can possibly get in the way of achieving goals is over-thinking. It is the individual's own responsibility to gain what one wants to accomplish in life. If one is willing to embrace a new approach to improving his/her life, the individual can reinvent life into something he or she truly wants.

SIX

Anxiety from the Past (PTSD)

Maria grew up in a very conservative family who used religion as a weapon for her parents' control. Everything she did was condemned in one way or another; so by the time she was fourteen years old, she knew she was going to hell. She heard statements like, "You are a slut because you came from sin, you were cursed from the day you were born from lust and the Devil's power, and you will be a whore forever, casting spells of your own."

Maria was not the only child who was accused of such wicked characteristics being the sister to three other children, but she was the oldest and the target of her parents' messages. She would counsel her younger siblings to disregard their remarks, but she never could develop any boundaries of her own to their criticisms.

As perhaps some justice occurred, both parents died of overdoses within a year of each other when Maria turned twelve, and she and her siblings found foster care to be a relief. By the time she was fifteen, her grandparents were serving as her home parents who showed love and acceptance abundantly and the story was beginning to emerge into her fantasy world of support and love.

Unfortunately, life doesn't go as planned and she was raped by a gang of drunken boys the next year. Being ashamed of the incident, she kept it a secret with the hope that she could avoid ever being hurt again; however, deep in her mind she heard her mother's voice of shame and ridicule.

As Maria began to mature into her intelligence and courage, she found school to serve as a level playing field and excelled in music. She had talents in an extraordinary wide range and quality for voice as the lead singer in a very prestigious high school for music and won many scholarships throughout the country. But something happened that was akin to the fantasy of the princess being saved by her prince when she met Tom in her freshman year in college.

Tom was the son of a very wealthy family and both he and his family fell in love with Maria almost immediately. Tom and Maria were married the first June during the summer break and Tom's family paid for all expenses of her college education as well as their living expenses for the remaining years of their education plan. Maria was on a golden road to fame, culture, and the best of the best life.

Although Maria could look at her life with amazing blessings, she kept hearing her mother's voice reminding her of her curses and status as a whore. She could not be happy but found that hours of psychotherapy could help her see the irrationality of her emotions; she could not keep her mind from hearing the voices of condemnations. The medications only made her numb and tired, and the walls of the institution they provided proved no resistance to the messages of lack of worthiness. In fact, what Tom and his family did for her made her more anxious because deep down she still felt like a whore. Maybe it was not as a sexual object, but perhaps because of her singing ability, her beauty, or even her remarkable intelligence that she felt she was being cared for. In her mind she was hexed and anything done in her behalf was dishonest compensation.

Maria found her own way of quieting the voice through alcohol. She discovered that she could find peace and fool herself a little longer with two vodka drinks in the morning and at noon, but it took much more at night to escape, usually drinking to blackouts and unconsciousness.

The next year was a disaster when she could not perform. It cost her the scholarships and any progress toward a degree, having to spend long periods of time in rehabilitation wards. Although the staff was competent, she was not able to remain sober. Her brain was inflamed with anxiety, alcohol, and self-hatred, and it became clear that her preferred state was being drunk. Sobriety was not a goal.

Maria's rounds with anxiety could be similar to the destructive pathways of PTSD memories caused with traumatic exposures to horrific experiences of warfare or the horrendous and gruesome agony of abuse of kidnapping and molestation, the memories that were the basis of her self-worth was contaminated with the constant assault of the auditory, and sometimes visual, implants of the messages of destruction. These do not go away with age, but may become more destructive in every path of life.

THE NEUROLOGY OF MEMORY RELEASE

Since the beginning of recorded philosophical history uniqueness of personality has been defined by our experiences of life events and our perception of their significance. From the *tabula rasa* of John Locke to the perceived sexual experiences of Freud, most psychological theorists have looked back into a person's history to explain one's neurosis. Alfred Adler even included one's selection of remembered life experiences, termed past recollections, to identify our distortions in our survival tendencies. Carl Jung brought forth the concept that humans not only react to their personal histories but also to their ancestors' with his concept of the collective unconscious.

Events with major personality consequences happen in a nanosecond. An abusive remark by a significant authority figure, a fall from a balcony creating a permanent disability, a demeaning insult at a vulnerable moment, or the remembrance of a peaceful picnic under a shady tree. People cannot remember all 2,459,808,000 seconds of our lives (based on a 78 year life expectancy), so they record those memories that are most significant. The life events that are remembered with emotional significance become one's internal life story thus determining one's destiny, both positive and negative.

The definitions of the depression and anxiety syndromes listed in the DSM-IV are specific in the underlying role that memory plays. For example, the ruminative nature of past memories erodes a person suffering from depression with destructive elements. In the recovery center, there is a common complaint among patients when they reach sobriety; it is "hearing my dad or mother telling me how worthless I am and that I will never amount to anything." Another common experience that serves as a basis for low self-esteem in the critical ages of adolescence is facing an embarrassing situation, such as the fourteen-year-old girl overhearing the boy she was going to ask to the dance telling one of his friends that he would not go with her if she asked because she was uglier than a mud fence. These memories can determine self-concept and even goal-setting for a lifetime.

Anxiety syndromes are even more explicit. PTSD is clearly defined as a trauma, experienced directly or indirectly, and kept in memory and re-experienced by cues and nightmares. Anxieties can be associated with fantasy memories or expectation, such as performance phobias and trauma (Dorfel, Werner, et al. 2010; Bryant et al. 2007).

Neurological Mechanics of a Memory

Like any other thought impulse, the process can be conceptualized as a shift or change in neuron excitement/activity that travels in various routes through the brain. When mapping the brain, the most clear is visual memory which occurs in the occipital lobe at the rear of the brain. This area lights up to clarify and magnify the visual stimulation from the sensory input; however, the pathways have to open up to the temporal and frontal lobes to identify the visual input and determine appropriate emotional responses. These processes have been explained in terms of chemical protein synthesis and electromagnetic rhythmic surges.

To qualify as a memory capable of recall, these neuron connections become more collaborative and develop a common firing sequence, which is called *coherence* in EEG readings (Principle I in Brain Plasticity). These are often referred to as long-term *potentiation* such that there begins an intricate cascade of automatic electrical firing of adjacent neuron cells.

Occasionally this potentiation can become powerful enough for the brain to create new receptors at the dendritic end of neurons, or an increase in the release of the chemical neurotransmitters that serve as communication enhancement between cells. Collectively the creation of a pathway that gains the capacity for recall and forms a part of automatic reaction to behavior is called the *consolidation* phase. The elaborate formulation of this neurological language was inspired by Jonah Lehrer.

In creating the major memory determinations one references for future behaviors, there are two distinct routes. The first is the learning process itself, which is usually a maturation of skill sets. The destruction of these linkages/pathways can be extremely debilitating, such as losing the ability to speak or walk. It can be disastrous to lose these memories, even if the goal is destroying negative emotions. The second feature that promotes the memory into present situations is routed through the amygdala (patients who have suffered damage to the amygdala are incapable of remembering emotions, such as fear). Again, as a caution to interfering with this association, it should be approached with sensitivity to the fact that both positive and negative memories form the perceptions of a person. Thus, for the person who is inspired to cure cancer by the memory of the suffering of a loved one would be detrimental to a life style of missionary service; however, the destructive aspects of self-loathing from a memory can be freeing and this section is focused on relieving the person from suffering of a destructive memory. Both features can combine for major coherence creating strong, vivid memories; however, it is the route through the amygdala that carries the emotional memory of greatest concern.

Until recently consolidation has been taught metaphorically as a blimp of experience that is stored in completed form and brought forth intact much like a computer file. However, Dębiec and his team of researchers clearly demonstrated that memories that are reactivated through retrieval become labile because they are interrelated in complex emotional networks, especially through the amygdala, rather than stored in isolation They tested rats by creating interlinked associative memories using a second-order fear-conditioning task and found that directly activated memories become labile, but using associative memories did not. The conclusions were that the disruptions of the fear emotion had to be closely associated in time for the response to be effective (Dębiec, Doyère, Nader, and LeDoux 2006).

Besides mental problems that can be related to destructive memory distortion, chronic pain has been implicated in memory programming. Fibromyalgia is a chronic pain syndrome that evolves numerous pain trigger points in muscles; this causes enormous discomfort and restriction of activities. There is no known cause or remedy for this disease that affects 2 percent of the population. One of the reasons for the mysterious etiology is that it is not limited to a set of tissues or predicted to an area.

Researchers at the University of Florida applied heat stimuli to the hands of healthy controls and fibromyalgia patients. In contrast to normal controls, fibromyalgia patients experienced a great amount of cumulative pain from these stimulations, indicating abnormalities in spinal cord pain processing. Furthermore, the fibromyalgia patients experienced residual pain when the stimuli were applied at intervals at which the healthy controls were not affected. Normally, pain sensations quickly subside after a single heat stimulus, but will accumulate with repetitions if they occur frequently enough. This "pain memory" appears to linger for an abnormally long period of time in fibromyalgia patients.

"Because the effect of the first experimental stimulus does not rapidly decay in fibromyalgia patients, the effect of subsequent stimuli adds to the first, and so on, resulting in ever increasing pain sensations," said lead investigator Roland Staud, MD. "Our findings provide evidence for abnormal central nervous system mechanism of pain in fibromyalgia patients and have significant implications for future therapies, which need to target these abnormal central pain mechanisms" (Staud, Vierck, Cannon, Mauderli, and Price 2001).

Erasing Emotional Content of Memories

Nader and his team of researchers made a major step in finding the clue to resolving destructive emotional content of memories when he stated, "Fear memories require protein synthesis in the amygdala for reconsolidation after retrieval"(Nader, Schafe, and LeDoux 2000). The researchers taught several dozen rats to associate a loud noise with a mild painful shock. After reinforcing the association over several weeks, he changed his methodology to injecting their brains with a chemical that inhibited protein synthesis and found that the fear memory was erased and evaporated from their behavior.

The disappearance of the emotional responses support the concept that every time humans try to remember something, the content is transformed by the emotional associations around it and possibly rebuilds itself every time they associate something new to it. This conclusion would make the behavior of the soldier with PTSD enhance the emotional complexity every time he or she relives the memory. It might explain why childbirth pain is rarely remembered; however, the positive aspects are remembered in loving and grand terms.

Similar research efforts have been done with human subjects. Beta-adrenergic blocker propranolol was administered after the retrieval of a psychologically traumatic event with subjects diagnosed with PTSD. The subjects (nine in experimental group and ten in control) received a one-day dose of propranolol during the memory. One week later, they engaged in precisely the same account. Physiological responses were significantly smaller in the experimental group (heart rate, skin conductance, left corrugator electromyogram) (Brunet, Orr, Tremblay, Robertson, Nader, and Pitman 2008).

Many studies have shown that the amygdala could be stimulated by electrically induced theta frequencies, which led the engineering to focus on the opportunity for the subjects to utilize the lower frequencies of 4–8 Hz. in the interference model (differences between the right and left ear). In reviewing the therapist data described next, it has been found the majority of the disruptor range noted as being the "2" range, which has been verified by the oscilloscope to be within the theta range the majority of the time (68 percent) for successful trials for all conditions.

Psychological attempts have been made in the arena of "thought-stopping" techniques. Although limited to novel experiences the act of yelling "stop" in the ears of the patient when involved with the imagery of a traumatic memory has been demonstrated with limited results. The behaviorists have recommended associating painful stimuli such as popping a rubber band on the wrist as a manner of dissolving unwanted memories. Aromas have the natural capacities to distract brain activities causing opportunities to disrupt memories, but no actual study has shown its long-term benefit. Certain types of biofeedback therapy protocols have shown decreased anxiety for specific memories and neuron-feedback protocols have even demonstrated changes in brain plasticity in reactivity (Gatchel et al. 1979; Plotkin and Rice 1981).

Sonic stimulation applied in a scientifically identified manner has displayed overwhelming results in the healing of traumatic memory. The next section will demonstrate my findings and introduces a device that has changed the way I treat patients.

The Sonic Application to Memory Desensitization

In an effort to utilize the concepts in destructive memory modification, sensory inputs appear to show great promise in altering brain focus on memory. The approaches were bound to the impact of strong aromas, mild electrical stimulus, and sound. The aroma therapies were too distracting and could not be controlled well enough. The electrical stimulation appeared to add fear and anxiety to the subjects rather than modify emotionality in memories. The sound stimulation was narrowed down to simple frequencies and well received by the subjects for self-regulation.

Recent preliminary studies by Rachel Bruursema of the University of Kansas Medical Center have shown in dealing specifically on the intervention of a spider phobia that the sonic frequencies (of the BAUD) do have effects on the higher activation in the left amygdala as well as left and right insula regions of the brain demonstrated by fMRI comparisons (Bruursema 2013).

Protocol for Release of Destructive Memories

Taking these principles in mind, a simple, self-regulating device was created, which has been affectionately referred to as the BAUD (BioAccoustical Utilization Device). The hero in this device is its simplicity of use and function as well as the potentiality of its application, rather than the device itself. In fact, a program has been created for an application for downloading that mimics the frequencies and functions of the BAUD, demonstrating the effectiveness of its principles and uses real-time hertz measures of the frequencies.

The device has only four controls: two volume knobs (one for each ear at 0–80 decibels), a frequency knob (frequency range of 36–360 Hz.), and disruptor knob (separation range 0–20 Hz.). The principle protocol for its application in the healing of traumatic memory involves four simple steps:

1. Adjust the volumes for each ear (0–80 decibels) for comfort. The sonic stimulation is harsh (square wave) because of the need to stimulate the amygdala and the brain components involving emotional issues. It may be seen as similar to an alarm clock that shocks the neuron-system. The more intense the better the result.
2. Rate the intensity of the emotion you are experiencing (fear, criticism, cravings, etc.) from 1 to 10, with 10 being the highest. Using the frequency knob, imagine the memory experience and its emotional association that you want to erase, and begin to find the frequency that is congruent with the emotion. Whatever rating given earlier, the rating of the intensity should increase. (This can be measured externally by physiological means, but self-regulation is best.) Note that this is the identification of the emotion and the sympathetic association to the experience.
3. With the frequencies set for the most intense level, use the disruptor knob to get a perceived reduction in intensity of emotion. This knob separates the frequencies between the two ears and creates an interference frequency in the balance sonically and neurologically. In our measures of parasympathetic states the brain quickly enters parasympathetic regions (skin conductance, heart rate, heart rate variability similar to the protein studies). The subject is asked for another rating of the intensity of their emotional issue.

4. If the procedure was successful, the subject is asked to continue to listen to the sonic stimulation and breathe long, deep breaths while holding the image of the experience. The usual response is either a difficulty holding the image/memory because it has lost its significance or a matter of fact memory with no emotional attachment.

Preliminary Results

As in any good theory construction, the concepts are only as good as the evidence. Since the conception of the theory of destructive memory resolution, there have been 410 identified health care professionals in fourteen countries (including The United States, South Africa, Puerto Rico, Israel, Netherlands, Canada, Australia, Namibia, and The United Kingdom) who have used the device in their practice. Of this number, 251 of these psychologists, neuropsychologists, and physicians were surveyed and returned data.

The purposes were focused on three main categories, emotional (anxiety and depression), urge or appetite, and pain or other physical symptoms. Within these categories, a multitude of problems have been treated. They responded to a general scale of how effective the protocol was in a range from poor (4 percent), fair (20 percent), good (40 percent)—identified as 50 percent of symptom resolved—and excellent, problem resolved (36 percent). The most significant finding was that anxiety related problems were resolved 100 percent of the time.

Besides the three categories, there were a number of problems treated successfully that expanded theoretical issues with possible destructive memory compensation behavior, such as the following:

- Reduce cravings to smoking
- Lose significant weight by reducing appetite cravings
- Pain—chronic to acute: post-operative, arthritis, tendinitis, carpel tunnel, dental, migraines, back, etc.
- Insomnia
- Adult thumb-sucking
- Eating disorders (anorexia-bulimia)

Surprising conditions that were resolved and are relevant to concept building were Parkinson's tremors reducing significantly in four individuals. One dentist used the protocol as a preventive measure before a dentist visit, targeting memory of previous visit pain, significantly reducing fear and pain.

In 2010, at the International Society for Neurological Research in Denver, Colorado, Lawlis reported on eighty-six patients treated by nineteen therapists in the United States, Switzerland, Portugal, and Denmark who underwent treatment for the resolution of destructive memory with the protocol and device before mentioned for one or more sessions. A Likert rating of symptom severity was recorded before and after treatment for all patients, and three weeks after treatment in a subset of patients. All were significantly improved with most having no more symptoms in three sessions or less.

An Improved Protocol for Addiction Issues

In an attempt to create a more sensitive protocol, a secondary set of steps were created based on the same psychoneuroplasiticity principles, which have shown a higher degree of success specifically among patients with addictions. The initial steps are identical to the basic protocol, with minor modifications in the "disruptor" step.

1. Adjust the volumes for each ear (0–80 decibels) for comfort. The sonic stimulation is harsh (square wave) because of the need to stimulate the amygdala and the brain components involving emotional issues. It may be seen as similar to an alarm clock that shocks the neuron-system. The more intense the better the result.

2. Rate the intensity of the emotion you are experiencing (fear, criticism, cravings, etc.) from 1 to 10, with 10 being the highest. Using the frequency knob, imagine the memory experience and its emotional association that you want to erase, and begin to find the frequency that is congruent with the emotion. Whatever rating given earlier, the rating of the intensity should increase. (This can be measured externally by physiological means, but self-regulation is best.) Note that this is the identification of the emotion and the sympathetic association to the experience.

3. After a brief resting period in which the person allows themselves to readjust the emotional state (called erasing the emotional board) instruct the client to adjust the disruptor (upper left) knob until the person finds some peace and relaxation emotions. Imagery may emerge that is associated with past pleasant memories. They often will find peaceful and joyous moments in their fantasies.

4. If the procedure was successful, the subject is asked to continue to listen to the sonic stimulation and breathe long, deep breaths while holding the image of the experience. The usual response is either a difficulty holding the image/memory because it has lost its significance or a matter of fact memory with no emotional attachment. The patient is asked to rate their levels of anxiety again to objectify their experience.

In summary, the protocol and concept of destructive memory resolution has at least one possible remedy using sonic stimulation. There are many implications and technologically creative improvements that have yet to materialize from this simple effort and articulation. More importantly, millions of people suffering from the symptoms of destructive memories can be helped efficiently and much less costly than the present options. For people like Maria, obtaining relief from such traumatic memories can open up a whole corridor of change. If Maria would have gotten a handle of her destructive memories, she could have gained her self-worth back and lived a rewarding life and continued her singing career building new pathways in the brain that are healthy. Since the past defines people, it is important that they are defined by experiences that are surrounded by peace so they can move forward and continue the journey they are traveling.

SEVEN

Depression and PNP Protocols

Delores appeared to grow up like any other girl, maybe a lot like her older sister, who set the stage for the family expectations. She did well in school, like her sister, and played flute well enough to make it to the "A" band when she was a freshman. She was pretty enough that she was not out of place with the "pretty" girl group and had plenty of the boys' attention. She was the ordinary girl who did what she did because it was the easiest way to be. She didn't cause trouble and avoided being singled out, even for positive contributions.

Delores was usually in the shadow of her older sister, yet she liked it that way. She did not want attention from others and certainly did not look for reinforcement from them in regards to her life or making life decisions. Her goals were uncertain, but life to her did sound challenging and exciting at times. She was labeled as a "floater" by her counselor.

So, as expected, Delores floated her way into a small college where she felt comfortable and it was here that her life would be changed forever. Within six weeks of school, she was hanging out with a group of friends who taught her how to get drunk and party, and for the first time in her life, she felt happy and normal. Delores was likely one of those people whose pleasure centers never get charged up and psychologically would have been diagnosed as "chronically depressed" or "dysthymia" (chronic mild depression). She was now experiencing something she had been seeking and that she had never known but had wondered what other people would get so excited about.

Delores would spend every week on some kind of drinking binge, even to the point of avoiding her family visits by being "sick" or "sleeping because of hard exams last week," whatever she had to do to hide the bags under her eyes and the suspicious loss of weight. Life was a joke and she felt she was finally in charge. Her class attendance dropped to three days a week, then to one, sometimes. By mid-semester, the dean sent her parents a letter that she was seriously in trouble academically, but any discussion was avoided with the explanation that "she was sick a lot and missed the important exams." She promised to do better, but she knew she was lying before the words left her mouth. She forgot to show up at her counselor's appointed time, as set up by the dean, because she had a bad hangover. In fact, she missed all of her classes and appointments because of bad hangovers or working on getting one.

By semester end she was fully into addiction, and there was no surprise to anyone. She was barely sober when the family moved her out of the dormitory and back into her childhood home where her trials in rehab would begin. She became cynical and oppositional to any help with more confusion in her mind as to her own control and what she wanted in life. Rather than put any effort into her own priorities, she let circumstances take the lead in her future, as long as she could drink to feel happy when she wanted.

Delores knew the steps in conformity because she had practiced it all of her life. She played the role of novice to the Twelve Steps three times in rehab programs, only to relapse two weeks after discharge. For her it was only two choices, to drink and be happy or to not and be depressed. For a nineteen year-old whose life had just begun, a lifetime of sadness was a bit much regardless of the health risks and a miserable future. Teenagers don't worry about the future anyway because their brains are pruning into special avenues and their ability to make judgments is pretty bad due to the underdeveloped frontal lobe, especially when understanding the future ramification of their behaviors.

THE NEUROLOGICAL MECHANICS OF DEPRESSION

Depression has been described as being the most destructive mental disease to humankind, largely because of the devastation it does to our lives and how it exacerbates disease, even to the level of suicide. Humans could set up their minds to ignore their feelings and barricade themselves from the pain of the brain pattern, and they could become like robots, not even considering the passion and joys that could be theirs. But then, they also might as well be dead if there is absence of passion, emotions, and feelings.

Much of the research into depression has not been very productive, especially as it pertains to addiction recovery. Studies that examine the "happy neurotransmitters" that transmit the joy experiences that humans perceive, such as dopamine, endorphins, oxytocin, and serotonin, indicate that they are interactive and usually involved with the addictive substances. This makes treatment difficult at best. There is also a lack of presentation of lab work to investigate whether these are relevant when a patient presents, making it hard to justify chemistry that is only noted by symptoms and not by physical measurement.

There are definite changes one can see and observe evident by brain scans. One of the most relevant of these efforts was reported in the National Academy of Sciences (Li et al. 2013) in which scientists from University of Michigan and lead author Jun Li, PhD, explained that every cell in our body, especially the brain, is connected to a circadian internal clock and related to how our bodies are governed. The circadian rhythm is the twenty-four-hour timing in which our morning functions shift to afternoon functioning to evening and night. These can be modified according to a person's personal schedules and needs. The main concept is that they exist in an integrated matrix, but there must be some coordination of the brain arranging all the functions of the body. For example, each organ has to restore itself onethird of the time or eight hours total. Even the heart has a rhythm in which during a heartbeat cycle, one third of the time is in restoration.

What was so important about this effort is the finding that people with the diagnosis of depression did not maintain the circadian clock integration and various regions of the brain appeared to be disjointed and operating on different time zones. This finding would explain why the symptoms are related to poor and shallow sleep cycles, confusion in the concentration, memory and cognitive features of the brain, and unstable emotional states.

The question might arise whether this lack of integration predates addiction or may be a feature of addiction detoxification, and that could be a future study; however, from the experiences of the PNP Center and part of this study, this is a factor that relates to depression alone, although by its definition given earlier, the disease of addiction is well known to alter brain patterns.

There are other ways to see the lack of rhythmic integration using the EEG, which measures electrical waves as described earlier. The classic brain pattern seen as part of the depressive emotions (and correlates very nicely with clinical analysis of melancholia depression) is one in which there's very low activity (alpha) in the left frontal area with expansion into the temporal lobes. The relatively higher activity in the right lobe creates a dominant left frontal lobe function, which then keeps you thinking in terms of less focus (Lawlis 2009).

When these mechanics of the brain timing and lack of integrated rhythms are happening, it just makes sense why a person with a low functioning left frontal lobe with slow activity to the temporal lobe would feel empty and irrelevant to emotional resolution. It would be predicted that people who have lost the joy and meaning in life might have the same or similar patterns. Men are especially vulnerable to shutting down their emotional life in order to succeed in objective pursuits, such as in business or relationships. Men's sexual interests also go by the wayside,

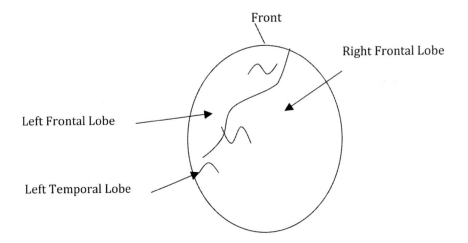

Figure 7.1.   Associated Brain Map to Depression

because they feel dead inside. If Scrooge were a real person, it might be argued that his brain pattern (pre-ghosts) would have shown his "joy centers" to be numb.

It is consistent with the thousands of evaluations done over a life-long career of dealing with people battling addiction who have nearly all reported that sometime in their history they've felt entirely unable to handle life's barrage of stresses and emotional demands, and their dive into substances were immediately related. Some were related to professional focus, but most of them related to an incomplete grieving process, whether it was a loss of a loved one, a relationship, or a job. They had all in one way or another "shut themselves down." And in the absence of a major inspirational experience or epiphany, they couldn't break away from the self-defeating, destructive pattern.

PROTOCOLS TOWARD JOY

The diagnosis of depression should be categorized into at least seven to upward of twenty different forms of despair and hopelessness because each person's experience, while sharing themes, is highly individualized within the area of the recovery process. There is evidence that depression can be inherited for either parent. The fascinating aspect is that just as the brain changes in cycles, these changes can create DNA changes. This means that if one is conceived during a depressive stage of the mother's or father's life, the DNA may be likely to be marked for the child, but not necessarily equally probable throughout their life time. In other words, the counselor may be dealing with genetic depression, but the good news is that this chronic state is not irreparable. Based solely on brain plasticity models these are the most effective approaches for rapid resolutions.

BAUD-Assisted Neurotherapy

By design, the BAUD device is a self-regulated approach to brain rhythm modification by what is known as entrainment principles. These principles simply state that the brain will begin to regulate its wave patterns consistent to those stimulating rhythms to which it is exposed. This principle will be discussed in later chapters and is the basic awareness that all of us have when musical patterns are consistently used to stimulate moods. For example, mood music can alter brain patterns and emotions for romantic shifts. Marching music has been used by the armed forces to shift brain patterns and emotions of unification of spirit and increase in physical endurance. Relaxation rhythms can induce sleep patterns, such as the tick-tock rhythms of a clock and the responding behavior of children and puppies alike to the rhythmic pulse of the heartbeat.

Protocol: The patient adjusts the volume knobs so as to produce a "loud" perception of the rhythms. It needs to be loud enough to trump any other rhythms of the brain. The second step is to have the patient use the frequency or "pitch" knob so that he or she feels a positive emotion or feeling. The patient may have to search for a few minutes, but there have been very few patients who fail to get some positive feeling; some even burst out laughing. The next step is to have the patient adjust the left upper "disrupter" knob as to increase the "joy" response. Some tweaking may be needed from there, but the main event is to have patients become aware of a way they can find joy and control their brains with positive thinking.

A note of interest: Since the patients have a sense of pleasure from their use of substances, they already have a perception of what that joy feels like. (Although, some chronically depressed patients have never known what joy feels like.) It would not be an inconsistent suggestion to their program to recommend that they find the settings that reproduce those feelings. These patients may use this strategy to substitute for their drugs and sonic methods are superior outcomes compared to toxic ones. This principle can be shifted into musical rhythms as well.

The EEG maps confirm that the brain patterns can be modified and integrated through sonic brain stimulation, and most important, the continuous use of the BAUD apparently normalizes into non-depressed.

Therapeutic training with neurotherapy is the most direct approach to dealing with specific brain patterns, and the particular unique protocol for the depressive brain constellation can be administered from any certified biofeedback therapist. Using the BAUD can accelerate the entire process of reaching the desired goals for brain function, and gives the patient a sense of control.

The process is similar for the Attention Deficit Stress Pattern. As the individual finds a frequency combination that appears to change the frontal and temporal lobes, the EEG predominant ranges are the SMR or Low Beta levels, they can use the BAUD whenever they want to increase their respective productive patterns. Over time, you may be able to do this process without the assistance of the BAUD; retraining the brain is the ideal goal and a likely outcome if practiced often over the course of time.

CD#2: Unity and Joy

In a similar attempt to modify the lack of coordination within brain rhythms, a CD was produced that had the theoretical beneficial rhythms of 60 hertz and was created by coordinating drumming sequences on a computer while adding live instrumentation. The instrumentation lasted twenty-two minutes and it is called "CD#2." The artist is Dr. Frank Lawlis, the creator of the mind body series online (MindBodySeries.com).

Not being a self-regulated device, it merely serves as a passive tool for a patient to use. Initially a group of severely depressed patients currently in therapy were asked to simply listen to the CD twice daily. Over a period of three weeks, the initial results astounded the therapists; however, although the patients acknowledge their impressive changes, they had no direct appreciation for the application but had no other explanation for their improvements. This observation has been proven consistent with further efforts to use the CD. The results appear subtle and take at least ten days to observe major differences and since these changes were at the brain level, it makes it hard to confine the event of improvement, although there has been no one who doesn't enjoy the CD and who does not continue to use it. The "musical" perception is that it is a pretty jazzy beat and many patients have danced and/or used it as part of their exercise. Children are especially happy to comply with its protocol.

Exercise

When it comes to mood improvement and depression, participating in physical exercise has been shown to be one of the most powerful (if not *THE* most powerful) behaviors to positively impact the mind and body compared to almost anything else people can do for themselves. However, some people take this to the extreme and exhaust themselves and their brains, which can do more harm than good. In a treatment setting, it is crucial to be watchful for any clients that may be partaking in any strenuous exercises regularly to be sure that the addiction pattern has not shifted into an unhealthy use of exercise. The secret isn't so much related to the amount of exertion, but rather, it's the rhythm of the body and breathing that does the magic. The benefits experienced by engaging in physical activity are practically instantaneous. And doing so on a daily basis helps a person sustain both the physical and emotional improvements immeasurably.

Horses have a natural way of coordinating the rhythm of their running because their lungs are like an accordion: As they run, their bodies squeeze and extend their diaphragm equal to their efforts. Humans are not built that way, obviously, so they have to train themselves into a rhythm. Some individuals consciously breathe in certain exercise patterns. When swimming, this occurs naturally because of the breathing patterns associated with the strokes (and not swallowing water). In walking, there is a purposeful control of breathing to the stride. It may be easiest to use music and sing along with exercise; it is also a lot more fun and the music can be inspirational as well.

Exercise is vital to the brain and uplifting to the emotions in many ways: it increases oxygen flow to the brain, it relieves the stress on the brain and body, it strengthens the brain's interactions and helps facilitate problem solving. Part of why this works is that it is believed that depression lifts because of the endorphin production associated with exercise. Commitment is essential, so if your client hates exercising, simply commit them to doing some very moderate physical activity (like walking in place and stretching) for just five minutes a day. One of the most interesting methods was described by a woman (who detests exercise in all its forms) who does something she calls, "commercial exercise." While watching television, she only exercises during the commercials. She will do curls with 5 pound weights during the first set of commercials, and switches to lunges for the second set. If she's feeling particularly motivated, she might do abdominal crunches. And when she has no motivation at all, she still does gentle stretches at every commercial.

Laughter

There isn't a scientist who wouldn't agree that brain patterns between sad and laughing people are different. Unfortunately, this protocol cannot be written with any conformity because the definition of great humor is lack of conformity with surprise comments and remarks about strange aspects of our world. Nevertheless, it would be inappropriate not to acknowledge this important venue in constructive brain patterns.

Many chronic patients have developed a tolerance and addiction to prescription pain pills. After they completed their original physical treatment program, they completed the required post-treatment exit interview as part of evaluating the best services, results and experiences possible. Nearly every patient rated the group support element and physical exercise programs as top-notch. But the patients who experienced the best success (as defined by them) were the ones who gave five stars next to "I learned to laugh again."

Learning a New Skill or Ability

Although it can be extraordinarily tough and difficult trying to convince someone who's in the depths of despair to concentrate on learning something new, it can also be a soothing remedy. For example, this old wooden flute, bought years ago, was musically idiot-proof. Each "note" is tuned to play a lovely chord. Patients loved to play this instrument because it always sounds good and it never failed to create an air of transcendence. Computerized pianos have the same concept with its chording systems. If patients appear emotionally stuck in neutral, they may want to try finding their own idiot-proof musical instrument.

Posturing

Mental health professionals know that one's body posture influences one's emotional state and vice versa (our body posture is an indication of our mental state). For example, if a person holds a standing position with the head stooped over, chest withdrawn, back bent forward, and eyes cast downward, the brain will soon follow, and that person will begin to feel miserable. However, if that person assumes a posture with the head looking straight out onto the world, the chest thrust out with the shoulders back, and arms spread open like wanting to give the world a big hug, it becomes far more difficult to hold onto a negative thought. Of course, that person can't maintain that posture indefinitely, but it's a fast and easy tool to get them unstuck. The work of Wilhelm Reich developed bioenergetics, a form of mind-body therapy. The idea behind current bioenergetic practice is that blocks to emotional expression and wellness are revealed and expressed in the body as chronic muscle tensions, which are often subconscious. The blocks are treated by combining bioenergetically designed physical exercises, deep exploration of body language, affective expressions, and palpation of the muscular tensions. Common terms in bioenergetics are breathing and grounding, in which a person is breathing continuously with their feet holding the ground firmly (Smith 2000).

Blue Lights and Chewing Gum

Interestingly, research has shown that brain patterns, such as the ones described for this brain storm, can be affected by having a blue light (25 watt bulb) shining toward the face for heightened brain energy activities. People of all ages have been shown to be positively influenced and enjoy better, more optimistic attitudes when exposed to blue light for fifteen minutes or more (Terman and Terman 2005). It's an excellent tool to embrace in the morning, if a person is not a "morning person."

The act of chewing may increase the blood flow thr
the brain associated with a brain storm pattern. In a
resonance imaging study, the regions of the brain
oxygenated blood were the sensorimotor cortex, s
area, insula, thalamus, and cerebellum (Onozuka, Fuji..,
no, Niwa, Nishiyama, and Saito 2002). Chewing sugarless gum ..
ly can wake up the brain. It also settles anxiety levels.

Nutrition

The motto is often right: you are what you eat, and nutrition is recommended as a front line offense to start on a high mental-energy diet. Probably the most significant factor for this particular pattern, and appropriate to all depressive states, is that changes in lifestyle are critical to changes in mental status. Chances are good that when a person becomes depressed, they will crave "comfort foods" dating back to childhood, which are sorely lacking in nutritional value. It's not unusual to visit someone at their home to find fast-food French fries, pre-packaged cakes and pies, pizza, and soda being the mainstay of food supply.

It's perfectly natural to want to eat those foods that our families gave us when sad and grumpy, otherwise known as "comfort foods." Consuming high-sugar, high-fat, nutritionally void foods are only going to send you deeper into your depression and possibly to overwhelming depths. For the few seconds of mouth pleasure, junk food truly is not worth it.

Supplements that are derived from foods have been shown to be very helpful in facilitating mood changes, especially bad ones. But remember, these supplements are truly powerful and may interact badly with medications you might be taking. Before introducing any of the following supplements into a diet, a physician probably should be consulted to ensure that the substances or foods considered are safe for you. Here are seven supplements with positive effects (Lawlis 2009):

1. *Rhodiloa* has been shown to have remarkable capacities to help moods and energy. Used in the Olympics as well as for space walkers for added strength; people have seen benefits in this pattern.
2. *Gamma-aminobutyric acid (GABA)* (dosage 200 mg taken four times a day) is an amino acid that appears to prevent the communication of depressing messages from nerve cell to nerve cell. This is like an anxiety management agent that neutralizes stress and serves as a powerful relaxing agent, which in turn keeps the system active in preventing resulting depression as an aftermath.
3. *Glutamine* (dosage 0.5–5 g. daily) is another amino acid that is converted into glutamic acid in your brain. The glutamic acid serves as a building block for proteins and nucleotides (RNA and DNA) that

stimulate the brain in the mood regions as well as elevating the GABA levels for stress management.

4. *Phenylalanine* is another building block for brain neurotransmitters that works directly with depression and sadness. It's also helpful in memory and alertness, but it can provide a real boost to libido. This can be found in almonds, avocados, bananas, cheese, cottage cheese, dried milk (nonfat), chocolate, pumpkin seeds, and sesame seeds. There are many precautions about using this substance with other drugs and physical conditions, such as hypertension, diabetes, and migraine. The recommended dosages are 500–1000 mg daily.

5. *Tyrosine* is naturally synthesized from phenylalanine and is a building block of several neurotransmitters, including dopamine, norepinephrine, and epinephrine. Since depression is associated with low levels of tyrosine, this is a natural recommendation. Tyrosine is a natural component in dairy products, meat, fish, wheat, oats, bananas, and seeds. As a supplement, label dosages range from 500 to 2000 mg; taken two to three times daily.

6. *5-hydroxy-tryptophane (5-HTP)* is seen as a precursor to tryptophan and serotonin, the neurotransmitters highly related to high levels of depression, anxiety, stress, and other moods of low mental energy. The general recommended dosages are 100 to 300 mg, three times daily. There are cautions if you are taking medications for depression, heart disease, or high blood pressure.

7. *Gingko-biloba* (120–240 mg. three times daily) is a favorite supplement, primarily from patient reports. It is believed to enhance the blood flow to the brain, specifically for the temporal lobes enhancement.

Twenty Qualities

For Delores (from the beginning of the chapter), since the time she was younger, she lived in the shadow of her older sister. Confidence and self-worth were concepts that did not live in her world and virtually were taught to be unimportant. As humans, happiness tends to be a concept measured by how much one can offer the world or society around them. Several studies have concluded that low self-concept is associated with depression in an inverse manner. For instance, as self-concept decreases, depression rates go up. Knowing one's strengths and building a healthy self-confidence is a skill that will allow depression to vanish. An exercise that will build this skill is to have the client write down twenty positive qualities that stem from intellectual, emotional, physical, and spiritual aspects of themselves. The statements must be in "I am" form. For example, if Delores felt she played the flute well, she would write down "I am musically talented." Once Delores found her twenty positive qualities, she would stand in front of the mirror and say each while keeping eye contact. Usually clients are told that this is a "rebirthing" experience because they are to embrace these qualities they will have in their recovered lifestyles. After repeating the qualities for forty days, the clients will become these qualities, provoking a sense of joy internally.

Stepping out of the depression trap isn't easy. Within the swirl of distractions and pessimistic forces, patients have to make a concerted, sustained, personal effort beyond anything they may have ever done. It's like taking those first steps with an 800-pound gorilla on one's back. It's very hard and there is the greatest of respect for those who have made those steps.

Other people have successfully made this journey time and time again. While they are all special people, there's nothing about them that is more special than one's individual story. Giving the client the direction of turning their own pages and changing his or her brain process represents the best of therapy.

EIGHT

The Delayed Adolescent Brain

By the age of sixteen, June was already on the streets prostituting herself for drugs and spending the little time and energy left looking for the next party. Day in and day out this was a never-ending cycle. She was introduced to drugs and alcohol by her father when she was twelve as his way of coaxing her toward sexual abuse. This went on until she left her home to live on the streets. When I met her, I saw what should have been a beautiful woman of twenty-five years of age but instead she looked about sixty due to the wear and tear of drugs, prostitution, street life, and the number of times she had been in trouble with the law and served jail time.

June had been in and out of rehab many times with the cycle of detox followed by sobriety until she found another party, which would turn into a series of more and more parties blurred into another few months on the streets. The one thing that June always used as her salvation was her high intelligence, seductive nature, and brilliant sense of humor. Regardless of the situation, she could always disarm people with laughter and assume a leadership position by creating opportunities for fun and stress relief. She was a likable person with a keen talent for finding fun.

In some ways, June was a program's worst nightmare because she was a force people loved to be around, and she could command leadership of a group in seconds. She knew the Twelve Steps by memory and even used them to create a comic script that could be played on Broadway. Needless to say, time and time again, counselors and staff were left frustrated.

June's only true goal was to make life a party. This motivation was directly related to the level of depression she kept underneath her smile. However, when her diagnosis was complete, hers was always "immature development" or "adjustment disorder." There are many Junes and male counterparts in the rehab system. These people can be problematic in that their immaturity seems to place them outside the ways of logic and respect of most therapies. They don't take seriously the concepts of transformation and rehabilitation and are just marking time until they can get on to their next party. Their brains appear to function at the level of age fifteen, which is the age of no responsibilities.

FINDING A PATH TO GROW UP

The concept of a standard approach for all drug and alcohol addiction has been debunked in several ways. Two classic personality studies have determined a multi-representation of at least three personality factors in a general population for alcohol abuse, and more could be added with the advent of additional drug combinations and socio-economic levels. Costello and Lawlis (Costello, Lawlis, Manders, and Celistino 1978) and Lawlis and Rubin (1970) demonstrated at least three major personality groups contained in rehabilitation programs. These were consistent with each other as having (1) a severely disturbed subpopulation that was highly toxic from the substance; (2) a "neurotic-like" group that was using drugs as a compensating management approach to anxiety and depression; and (3) a fairly normal group who had bad habits of drug use.

In dealing with brain barriers, it appears that these persons suffer from what is coined as "chronic adolescent brain syndrome." This is based on the current observation that many of drug rehabilitation patients score high on the PsychEval Personality Questionnaire (PEPQ published by IPAT) pathological scales of high need for "Thrill Seeking" and low "Threat Immune" tendencies. These scores can be interpreted as a high need for excitement and a low fear of authority that are consistent with levels of immaturity. The act of marijuana abuse is also correlated with these factors.

These immune judgments have been demonstrated in a gambling task administered to a group of cocaine abusers by researchers headed up by Dr. Vicki Nejtek at the University of North Texas University Health Science Center (Nejtek, Kaiser, Zhang, and Djokovic 2013). The task involved the selection of cards from four decks for gambling for profit. Decks A and B were cards with high payoff but high risk for losses; whereas, decks C and D were cards with lower payoffs but fewer losses. The selection of cards and performances were related to the frontal cortex and showed poor judgment and assessment for payoff.

In the observation of the relapse patients, it has been remarkable how difficult it is to adequately prepare them for their needs for excitement and risk that they have been fulfilling with their use of stimulants. The fact that most of these patients usually come from the eighteen to twenty-five years of age grouping makes sense because their brains are naturally going through the pruning process and rebellion toward tradition is common.

ISSUES WITH "DELAYED FRONTAL LOBE DEVELOPMENT"

The abusive behavior with assortment of drugs usually starts as early as the age of twelve and is associated with parties and other rebellious behaviors of early adolescence. Although there are little differences in sedative and stimulating drugs, their purposes are usually set as social connections and inductions into social groups.

Part of the frustration is that this stage of development for the brain is considered normal for all of us. These are the years in which people lose judgment, especially the importance of ramifications of their behavior on their future (Steinberg 2004). One's physical reactions are actually increased and their physical abilities are magnified, making them the strongest and quickest they may be in their lives. Sexual and passionate motivations are the highest, at least for males, and their sensitivities grow stronger daily. It is also true they become a degree less smart; at least in those subjects in which they have the least talent. That is the reason the armed forces focus on this age group. They feel invincible to debt and will do most anything they feel is exciting (Dahl 2004).

But this may be an abnormal state; it usually subsides and passes for the most part by the time a young adult has to go to work as a responsible citizen. It is the ones who have a delayed state and maintain their priorities to be our Peter Pans who can't escape this vulnerable time for addictions.

PSYCHONEUROPLASTICITY APPROACHES

One of the primary functions of the frontal lobe of the brain is to organize and learn the critical components of how to survive and to thrive in an intellectual world. Our academic experiences stimulate and develop the brains so that humans can create language and methodologies to understand more information that is relevant to their goals and aspirations.

When the frontal lobes of our brains are damaged, which is very prevalent in automobile accidents, sports injuries, and many teen activities, one of the signs of injury is the inability to learn new information and organize materials. For example, when given the task of using construction blocks to reassemble forms and shapes, they do poorly. They can't solve even elementary problems, and as the research noted above, they have poor judgment about their resources.

Our educational system is given the mission to educate the masses, and like our personalities, our brains are individualized. Otherwise, stimulating our brains would be direct and our frontal lobes could be mass produced by stimulating it into productivity. Since there are individual pathways to styles of learning, there is more than one way of stimulating the brain into new circuits. There are basically three ways of cognitive stimulations in learning: (1) abstract or deductive/inductive reasoning; (2) rote memory in which people learn by memorization; and (3) trial and error. Cognitive approaches make use of all three methods.

Consider June's case in which a more abstract method was imposed. June was asked why she was still thriving on the party-high feeling, and although being very bright, still selling her body. She replied that although she loved the attention of men, she loved the control more. She went on to explain that men were like her father, and that she felt that she was actually taking sexual advantage of their weak wills. There was a thrill of getting them drunk and taking their money.

June demonstrated that she had the articulation skills to be a candidate for cognitive restructuring and was asked what other activities would meet these same needs. This process took a couple of hours but proved very fruitful. She discussed the idea of gaining control as a teacher where she could learn how to serve children by instructing them on being healthy. She also discussed the idea of an acting career but felt distance between her and an audience in this role. Counseling as a profession was considered because of her need to help people. Many other vocations were considered, but through the process of discussing her change in work activities in meeting her goals, she displayed a "cognitive flexibility" in opening up to real possibilities in solving her emotional needs through a more constructive life plan.

Although she amused herself with several alternatives, she settled on one avenue she witnessed in a trial. She was excited about the role of doing mock trials for lawyers. Using her seductive abilities she got her chance in two months from our discussion and has earned several contracts since then. As vocational guidance, this line of work for her would appear as a misfit, but it fit her goals like a glove.

The director of a mock trial sets up a preliminary trial, using one or two representative juries and real witnesses. A judge is employed to rule the process as if it were a real trial. As the process goes, the witnesses are judged as to how effectively they present their side as well as the lawyers' performance and the quality of their materials. The substitute holds their meetings and decides on a verdict. The idea is that the lawyers get to perform and get advanced feedback in order to maximize their side, and it may take several runs to make it right in order to achieve the desired jurist's reaction.

June found her passion and exercised her various strengths of intelligence, seduction, and creativity to develop a more constructive lifestyle for her than her former destructive end. In addition, this line of work was thrilling and provided the party-high feeling she craved. Moreover, she retrained her brain to accomplish more pleasure and power for herself.

She had to learn new terminology, but more importantly she learned a new place for herself in the world.

RETRAINING THE BRAIN THROUGH DIRECT MEMORY

Not every adolescent user is as smart and flexible as June, but there are many other avenues. For example, Eikeen was a man with an extremely dark past of drugs and was already looking for a party while still being processed out of rehab. Eikeen knew very little about life but knew much about poverty and jail time. When he was interviewed for the first time, it was hard for him to admit that he had any opportunities to live a different life, and he felt the only way in his life that he could feel good about himself was through drugs. He was wrong.

As described in earlier chapters a process called "Twenty Qualities" is recommended for these individuals where they have to find at least twenty positive qualities upon which they know they can survive. Upon listing these twenty-plus positive perceptions, they are to recite them daily for forty days looking into their own eyes in a mirror, as a ritual of looking into their soul.

Eikeen was resistant at first and could only think of seven positive qualities, but he was encouraged and he persisted and added more for a total of twenty-eight qualities. The staff started addressing him as "28" and pointed out these positive qualities as they observed him. (Note: This name changing is an inherent process in which self-identities are often changed radically and associated with this study into using brain patterns to shift self-esteem. Too often our identities are related to another's name, such as a parent or relative and the child is to be sentenced to a life of either shame or stand-in. Many "juniors" have suffered lifetimes under the identity of someone else.)

"28" was later replaced with "TE" short for twenty-eight. TE changed before our eyes. He walked differently. He talked differently. He demonstrated these positive attributes every day, and was reborn personality-wise. He reached his certification as a drug counselor and serves with great distinction in one of our nation's premiere drug programs.

The process of retraining the brain to recognize his true humanity gave him a sense of responsibility to serve that profile he now knew in his heart to be true. Perhaps this can be akin to using a mantra (a sacred word or phrase that one repeats to oneself such as "I am important") to guide one's actions or the transformation of a human mind. There is such a thing as being reborn into your true self and it is proven every day in the treatment of addiction through psychoneuroplasticity.

TRIAL-AND-ERROR PROCESS

By and large, most of people are trial-and-error researchers in life. They test it to be sure and to see if it is good. Women kiss a lot of frogs before they find our princes. Humans ask questions and try out relationships, drugs, food, jobs, and self-concepts. People make progress by making mistakes. This approach takes much longer for the drug addict to change his or her frontal brain development.

Brian was a good example for this approach. He had a very detailed memory that served him well. He was one of those people, who at the age of twenty-eight, was still going from one episode of trouble to the next, stealing cars, getting into accidents while under the influence, getting into fights, and so on. It could be said that he suffered from *affluenza*, a fake diagnosis which relates to being spoiled by his family and enabled to get away with many infractions, always being rescued by his family's influence.

When the discussions became truthful, Brian would admit that he was spoiled and was actually resentful of his situation because he knew he was treated differently from his friends. On a deeper level, he was anxious because he felt he had no boundaries to his behavior, and his family did not care enough to treat him like an adult. Much of his problems may have been an attempt to gain attention and prove he was an adult.

Brian began to work on the goal of gaining control over his life, and the course of action was to let go of allowing others to control him. Being latent of brain development, he was added to hyperbaric chamber healing and exercise was added to his daily schedule, but the day-to-day counseling received the most attention. These sessions took the form of a series of exercises or experiments. For example, he created a "bubble of influence" around himself and went through a list of questions for every thought he had, challenging them as being reliable and valid. If he felt angry because someone directly or indirectly hurt his feelings, he would ask himself these questions:

1. Were my feelings based on fact or opinion? If they were fact, then they were empirical and could be proven without conflict. If they were opinion, then they couldn't be proven, so they could be valid or invalid.
2. Were the statements dangerous to my health or lifestyle? If not, then they could be dismissed. If so, they had to be entertained and acted upon.
3. Were they part of my reality or someone else's? If someone else's, then could they be irrelevant? If they were part of his, then he might need to listen for educational sake.

It could be said that these questions might be incomplete, but the issue is twofold. Staff wanted Brian to stop and review the issues on a rational basis, and they wanted him to have some set questions in his mind. This was not automatic either. It took several trials to implant these phrases into his thinking, especially when he was emotionally charged. He was given a strong aroma (peppermint) in a bottle to smell and reset his mind, which helped, and he used counting to ten for the same reason.

As he started pausing and thinking through the situation, he began to get rewarded with quarters. Quarters do not buy much, but they are heavy and shiny and they are earned.

PROGRESSIVE IMAGERY

Imagery is an ability these types of people have in abundance. They love to daydream of many fantasies and adventures. By using one's fantasies, real-life scenarios can be played out with similar outcomes in life. For example, you can decrease the number of training sessions it takes someone to learn to fly an airplane by having them visualize the processes it takes to fly using their imagination. It is amazing how the mind can create real-life outcomes.

It has been shown that learning sports, such as tennis or golf, through imagery allows one to learn faster than only using direct instruction (Sheikh and Korn 1994). The imagined experience teaches the body to integrate the action at least 50 percent as well as direct instruction. It was discovered that when teaching surgery patients rehabilitation exercises and observing/imaging the process in recovery, they did not suffer as much atrophy in their muscles.

The process goes similarly with addiction and can be enhanced when done in groups.

1. The individuals are asked to imagine personal situations when they feel most vulnerable to using drugs. The usual approach would be to take the three most vulnerable situations; however, only one situation should be approached per session per individual.

2. After the situation is selected (each person can have different situations at the same time), the group takes a few moments and imagines the situation and examines their feelings and emotions. Then a discussion follows in which the situations are assessed in terms of underlying factors, such as history and context.

3. The next phase is when the group goes back into a relaxation state and imagines at least three different constructive reactions that would be expected to resolve the need to take drugs. These are termed the hypotheses resolutions.

4. An open discussion is held among the group (or with a counselor) and these ideas are brought to some objective view. They are modified or others can be added in order to be helpful.

5. With refined options, the individuals are encouraged to try these solutions out in their imagined scenarios, one resolution at a time. It is interesting that if a solution is not reasonable in reality, the imagery also tends not to be realistic. This is similar to mental rehearsal used in military training.
6. The solutions attempted are reviewed in the group (or with a counselor) as to how successful they were in the imagination state. Usually there are some modifications inherent in the trials or some are replaced with new ones. That is the way the brain works.
7. With some discussion about the discovery of imagined trials, the sessions are terminated and new situations are brought up for the same process.

There are many examples to share but the one that stands out is Lucille's, due to her unique ability to unify her actions around her pets, especially her dog, Prince. She noted that she felt most vulnerable to abusing alcohol when she was afraid of failure. Apparently, she grew up with a mother who impressed upon her daughter that success was everything and the worst of labels was "loser." Being rather talented in the music field, she was placed in competitions early in life and developed a performance anxiety that included everything beyond her musical pursuits.

Lucille would compete for attention, for academic status, for beauty, even how well she could sleep. Actually she was a poor sleeper and worried every day whether or not she would get a good restorative sleep. Alcohol became one of her ways of dealing with sleep, and eventually everything else.

Lucille created three options for her anxiety issues besides alcohol: talking to her dog, taking a walk, and doing breathing exercises. Talking and touching her dog was interesting on multiple levels. Her dog was the epitome of unconditional love, something she wanted from her mother, and it also gave her a chance to touch fuzzy texture, which she loved and allowed her to get grounded. During the group discussions, these attributes were brought up, but what was also noted was that Prince was not always around. Her solution was to carry his collar with her.

MEDITATION EXERCISES

There are many forms of meditation and the one that appears to have the greatest success according to our observation will be presented here. The most powerful and relevant to brain frontal function is what is referred to as "mindful meditation" (Hölzel, Ott, Hempel, Hackl, Wolf, Stark, and Vaitl 2007). Generally speaking, mindful meditation is focusing on present stimulations and sensations in the immediate awareness. Mindful meditation starts out with diaphragmatic breathing and paying attention to the inhale and exhale of each breath. After finding rhythmic breath, meditators are to observe their mind with no judgment, simply noticing and embracing each thought, feeling, or emotion that comes up during their mindful meditative experience. Meditators are told that staying in the present is the only time one is actually living and to experience all senses while living in each moment to moment is a powerful experience that satisfies the brain (Cahn and Polich 2006).

What happens so often for people in addiction is that they immediately rationalize the result of a situation quickly, too quickly, to consider alternative outcomes. They become fixated on stressful consequences and immediately build up resistances. For example, Debbie would be told that her boss wanted to see her, and immediately she would build up anger because she projected that it would be like going to the principal's office in school for something that she didn't do or that she did wrong. In a matter of fifteen seconds her attitude would nosedive into anger and depression that would manifest into stubbornness and cussing, out of control behavior. Her stress would immediately turn to wanting to rebel like a teenager, so her first immediate behavior would be to light up a cigarette, then make up an excuse to leave work and get drunk. Being a good worker, the boss always was complimentary, but she never heard it.

As Debbie began to practice feeling every mini-second of what she was experiencing (and it did take practice since her thinking was so reflexive), she began to enjoy more of the immediate issues in her life rather than the past and future ramifications. She would focus on how it felt to walk barefoot, how the sky looked at different times of the day, how it felt to walk with someone else, how every bite tasted when eating a biscuit or an apple. There was a decrease in trying to overreact to situations and over-interpret what other people felt.

Debbie started to allow life to be a mystery and appreciate the good times. There was even a time when she could expect bad events, but these were short-lived instead of taking over a week or a month to resolve. She finally resolved to herself that negative events did not have to preside over her life for more than it took for them to happen. There were more good things that could happen than bad, and if she paid attention, there would be at least 100 times more good things that happened to her than bad.

Perhaps it was the issue of control over life as becoming internal that resulted from mindful meditation. Perhaps it has been an opening into the theater that happens in our mind's eye that gives new perspective. Whatever it is, it works.

THE VISION QUEST

Whatever process the adolescent mind is going through, it is usually going through the question of what life will be about. Is there a specialty mission where one will dedicate their lives? It can be becoming a husband or wife, a parent, a professional, and so on. This concept of the future is what directs a young mind to make priorities as the brain develops into special talents and abilities.

However, if there are no ambitions or visions of the future, the mind has no goals and becomes stagnant. Perhaps that is the reason for lack of growth beyond the rebellious mode of beer busts and pot-smoking ventures of adolescence into adulthood, middle age, and even into the elderly years without growing up.

In many cultures there are rituals through which young adults go through to designate their special purposes. In the United States there are secondary schools to help sort these out, at least vocationally. Not having any immediacy to the process, our culture has moved the reality of an action plan back to college or military service. Various religious organizations have kept the spiritual component to early adolescence, which may be a little out of sync with brain development in this time generation. With the physiological rhythm coming earlier and with our world in a very complex transition, changing from generation to generation, these rituals are being left behind. However, they have been designed to help the brain understand itself and find direction through the chaos of life. To add to the problems of these tasks at this critical time of life are the impacts of drugs on the brain.

The "vision quest" ritual has been described in many ways and in its most traditional format was an experience in which the young warrior was either sent out into the forest with only a weapon and water, or he was taken into the forest or range and, with only water and a blanket, would remain there for three days. In either case, the object was to have an experience in which a totem would communicate with him and give him a "vision" of what his immediate quest will be. Upon returning to his community his duty would be to explain his quest by creating a dance, song, story, or symbol of some kind in honoring of the experience.

The availability of forests is usually hard to find, especially without some danger associated with being alone for a time, although these are being carried out today. The main objective is to create a separation in consciousness from an ordinary state of mind (Harner, Mishlove, and Bloch 1990) in which open imagery can be enjoyed. This means there is no intention to visualize anything but to allow images to come to the person between thoughts.

Vision Quest Protocol

The first requirement is to find a suitable place, which would be free of cell phone sounds, interruptions, and external stimuli. The instruments are given in the beginning and only the timed signals interfere with the process.

The process is simply an opening in your consciousness in which some symbol may arise in your experience. It may be an animal, a plant, a color, a spiritual figure, or anything that you can relate to. You will imagine a journey. The first part of the journey will be a search for a river or body of water. Next to the water will be a boat. You will climb into the boat and lie down, allowing the boat to take you somewhere. It is during this time that you relax and let the boat travel to whatever destination it wants. You can feel the waves beat against the boat as it continues its path. Let the motion relax you more and more.

Soon enough the boat will stop and come upon a shore. This is your time to step out of the boat and see the wonderful view of a wooded area, full of plants and butterflies and birds. Wander around and observe the scene and feel welcome. You will come to a bench. Sit down and wait for your symbol to appear. It may simply walk up to you or call your attention to it.

As it appears, welcome it. You may talk to it, but the communication may be only telepathic. Listen and observe. The message may be symbols or actions. Feel the messages and open yourself to more symbols.

After about twenty minutes, I will signal you that it is time to return. When that happens, bid farewell to the symbols and figures who have met you and find the boat that brought you here. Enter the boat and have it bring you back. Open your eyes when you come back here.

It is recommended that a drum rhythm accompany on the journey at a rate of 4–5 beats a second. This rate approximates the theta frequency of the brain which is associated with high imagery and deep relation, making it easier to engage the imagination. It is also easier if the participants are lying down or sitting such that they do not have to compete with gravity as they relax their bodies.

While processing the experience both the communication that is remembered and the meaning of the symbols are important to the question about life quest. For example, if the symbol is a horse, it has significance as a symbol of power. If the symbol is a beaver, it has symbolic value as a virtue of working intently and building things. It may be important to have a dictionary of symbols, especially of animals (Andrews 2010).

For a young mind these symbols are important to help the mind conceptualize the life quest because the symbol has many layers of importance (Lawlis 1996). For example, Shawn saw a triangle with a snake, which meant that the triangle was the mountain he needed to climb for his healing, but in order to climb a mountain he would need to dislodge the baggage he was carrying.

Once the participants had an understanding of their journeys it would be good for them to create a song, picture, dance, or other construction to integrate the symbols in their mind and life. Mental investigation as well as psychological emotional counseling would be helpful to clarify one's mission.

SUMMARY

Engaging the mind of an immature person who has been on drugs can be a frustrating experience, especially if that person appears to be unable to deal with a logical or rational framework. Also, for some reason there is stubbornness in the brain that resists external guidance. This is normal in that the mind is searching for personal meaningfulness, not logic, and to the addict the world is chaos. The easiest method of dealing with it is through the use of drugs and sex, not struggle.

It is the struggle that must be endured and confrontation is not bad, only condemnation. Encouragement to struggle and work hard is made, and this includes physical work. The energy of this age must be channeled, not subdued, and these experiences can help grow the brain in healthy directions. However, this stage of life is full of question and regret, due to the trial-and-error mode in which the brain engages. Patience and perseverance are important elements on both sides of the desk.

NINE

Depression with Intruding Messages (Rumination)

Pat was the oldest of three girls and like so many other oldest sisters, she felt the responsibility of the family's reputation, the younger sisters' welfare, and her mother's health. According to her mother's daily sermons, Pat knew how a home was supposed to be run. Pat did not rebel with all this responsibility. In fact, she enjoyed the notion that she had more power than her siblings and more respect from her mother for being more of a "helper" than a daughter.

Pat's life became more complex when her stepfather also seemed to consider her more than a daughter, and although the boundaries of molestation were never broken, there were transgressions that made her feel strange and compromised, such as when he would walk around naked (when her mother was not home) and ask her to touch him (inappropriately) because his hands were occupied or the many other excuses he made up. He continuously made sexual comments and asked questions about what her understanding was about sex and he would "accidentally" open the bathroom door when she was taking a bath and hold it open while he asked a question. She would often find him going through her drawers and "checking to see if they needed to be washed."

Pat had a feeling of guilt largely because when she tried to address these problems with her mother, she would quickly dismiss them and treat Pat like she brought up a bad topic or had done something wrong. But there was the wonderment of why a grown man would have any interest in a young girl like her, yet she knew this should not be happening. As a way of dealing with her guilt she became a perfectionist house keeper to control her mind from the building anxiety she was dealing with. When she would get things very clean and tidy, her mother praised her with rewards and her stepfather would hug her with much affection in sight of everyone, making it seem okay to receive such well-deserved affection.

Fast forward the time line twenty years and Pat is still cleaning to perfection in order to relieve her anxiety, but now she also has the voice in her head of her mother's comments and how she must live up to her expectations. This mental process is much like the PTSD brain traps, only there is no trauma to respond to, only ruminations in her head and a learned behavior that makes her life miserable and has no built-in reinforcements, such as hugs and praise. The lingering guilt over being deceptive to her mother and secret pleasures of her stepfather's attention made her depressed and ashamed.

The complicating emotions grew stronger every day. Pat knew she needed help and sought the advice of several professionals, including her pastor, two psychologists, a psychiatrist, and a family therapist. She could not admit her memories to her pastor and felt they were too complicated to explain to anyone. She was diagnosed by her psychiatrist with obsessive compulsive disorder, but the medicine for anxiety only deepened the ruminations and guilt.

The use of addictive substances is very similar and its end results are the same. As could have been predicted, Pat started using alcohol and cocaine to deal with all the guilt and so that she could actually embrace her "sexual naughtiness and rebellion." She had a community of drug dealers and users who obliged her promiscuity and she almost felt the pleasure of the earlier hugs and attention from her stepfather. This was her escape from the living hell and torture of her mind.

DEPRESSION WITH RUMINATION

The ruminative depressive cycle has been described as "living a hell on earth," being condemned by God with guilt and by one's family for being obsessed with unimportant things. The feeling is one of a circle of forces that keeps turning the memories of the brain around and around, so the patient keeps finding himself back where he started. It is hard to fight it because the self-confidence has been broken. One feels like a victim of psychosis, but it is opposite in the sense that one cannot escape internal reality and if one were psychotic he or she would escape it altogether, which is why these people turn to drugs and alcohol so often.

A Picture of the Brain and Ruminative Factors

A representative drawing of a brain SPECT Scan pattern is presented in Figure 9.1. A fascinating aspect of this picture is that the image of the post anterior segment of the *cingulated gyrus* (the rounded ridges on the brain's outer layer) is clearly visible as having a very high activity level.

The anterior cingulate cortex (ACC) looks like a collar around the corpus callosum, which is a rainbow-looking nerve bundle that connects your brain's two hemispheres. It appears to not only play a role in coordinating higher cognitive functions, such as focusing on different parts of the brain and integrating their perceptive values for optimal problem solving. It also facilities one's ability to identify with other people's emotions (i.e., empathy) and coordinates emotional responses. (Paul, Brown, Adolphs, Tyszka, Richards, Mukherjee, and Sherr 2007).

Additionally, a team of researchers (Allman, Hakeem, Erwin and Nimchinsky at Cal Tech) demonstrated the capacity (and even the survival) of these functions can be profoundly affected—either positively or negatively—by environmental conditions such as enrichment or trauma (Allman et al. 2001). Additionally, according to research conducted by Alcino Silva and colleagues at the University of California, the anterior cingulate cortex (ACC) is involved in modifying new memories into permanence. To implicate this vital component further into the topic of rumination disorders, there's considerable evidence suggesting that a major role of the ACC involves conflict monitoring (Frankland, Bontempi, Talton, Kaczmarek, and Silva 2004).

ACC's role in new memory storage may also explain why this function is associated with post-traumatic stress disorder (PTSD). It makes sense that if someone is exposed to a traumatic event and their ACC gets damaged, it could get stuck on "replay" in such a way that keeps the person experiencing the event like it's actually happening for the first time all over again (like déjà vu) as opposed to simply remembering an event which fades over time in both intensity and detail. This concept may also help explain the repetitive obsessive memories in obsessive

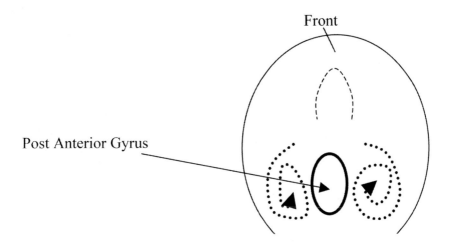

Figure 9.1.   Associated Brain Map to OCD

compulsive disorders, for example, perhaps a person keeps doing things like repeatedly checking the door locks, because the memory of performing the task is somehow repeatedly deleted as well. Thus, the brain insists that the task must be performed again.

PROTOCOLS

The rumination depressive syndrome may not be unique to addiction, but it can and often does serve as a barrier to sobriety. As in Pat's story, the trap within a person's brain can only be released momentarily through drugs, the mental pain and frustration to the freedom will be used repeatedly to death. The choice of living within that depressive disease and a drunken state is not hard to understand and creates a major life-long decision. However, through the use of brain plasticity the process can be quicker and under the patient's power and control.

It should be remembered that the barrier contains two conflicting emotional reactions, anxiety and depression, and may be immune to psychological reasoning, at least until rational reasoning is possible. Also, the histories for everyone are different, making the protocol very unique in intensity and outcome.

BAUD

A special application of the BAUD can be used for neutralizing high emotional triggers. For Pat, the guilt from the duel onslaught of a mother's messages for morality through cleaning and her stepfather's sexual overtures were major triggers. She imaged a past emotionally-charged situation of her stepfather's seductive actions with the overtones of her mother's sermons as the arousal of her sympathetic system. Similar to the PTSD protocol, Pat slowly turned the upper right knob (frequency/pitch) of the BAUD until her emotions were at their peak. This is a process in which the frequency is found that actually stimulates the anxiety/depression response. In Pat's case, as she kept the visual image of her stepfather in her mind and the auditory voice of her mother, she slowly moved the frequency knob on the BAUD until she felt the surge in her emotions. She became increasingly angry and upset. This was the frequency she found for the setting that best correlated to her lightning stress.

The next step is finding a secondary frequency that neutralizes the high-anxiety frequency and the emotional response as well. Pat was instructed to the imagery for a moment and used the upper left knob (disruptor) to find a harmony that pleased her. This knob created a separation in the two tones and found a setting that neutralized her emotional reaction. As Pat moved the knob she stopped with a smile on her face. The two frequencies had cancelled the emotion and she felt a sense of

calm. Interestingly she saw an image of her first birthday party and seeing all of her friends celebrate her day. On follow up visits she reported
an absence of her emotional memory and her birthday party.

What the BAUD is accomplishing is neutralization. In essence, it's a
method that uses contrasting frequencies to cancel out the emotional
brain response. What is particularly fascinating is that in most cases
when the sympathetic (arousal) and parasympathetic (relaxation and restoration) measures (such as heart rate variability and muscle tension) are
monitored, the patient has an immediate shift when the neutralizer frequency emerges: The heart rate variability becomes steady and the muscle tensions release! In Pat's situation, she felt immediate relief from the
depression and anxiety.

The individual uses the device to stimulate the brain region, in this
case, the cingulated gyrus. Once the frequencies are seen as accomplishing this objective, the individual can take the BAUD anywhere he or she
goes. If a storm is triggered, the device can be immediately used to swift-
ly achieve brainwave regulation. This can be accomplished in one or two
sessions, and with continued training provides even greater efficacy.

Smell

One of the ways to have the brain pause from its cycles is to have the
patient take a couple of deep inhalations from a powerful smell, such as
clove or peppermint. In neurology, one quickly learns that the olfactory
sense has more immediate connections to the brain than touch, vision, or
auditory stimuli. With this advantage, it has more immediate effect on
the brain and will trump any other action, including higher emotional
ones. If the patient can't seem to get out of the irrational reaction to their
triggers, simply have them close their eyes and take a couple of whiffs of
their chosen favorite fragrance. Whatever emotional turmoil was going
on will be immediately cut-off, giving them time to reset their emotional
cycles in order to associate some relaxation suggestions.

Biofeedback and Aromas

One avenue to the brain pathway that is interesting in is the olfactory
system. The fact that the olfactory system is the only one that connects
directly to the brain instead of traveling to other areas of the brain is
incredible. While other sensory processes travel along the thalamic route
to the primary cortical region that processes the sensory information, the
olfactory system travels directly to the forebrain. In other words, the
effect of an aroma can be instantaneous and provoke a direct neurological
and psychological effect on a person. When an aroma is smelled there are
10 million olfactory cells, each of which has 350 different receptors in the
nose that communicate with the olfactory cortex, amygdala, and hippo-

campus, which stores memories and emotions. These receptors are each specialized to distinguish particular aromas. There are also researchers that believe that smelling essential oils stimulates parts of the brain that influence physical, emotional, and mental health. Aromas have been used for therapeutic purposes for nearly 6,000 years. Essential oils were used for spiritual, therapeutic, and ritualistic purposes in Egypt, China, India, and Rome. The Chinese were the first to use aromatherapy with the use of incense to create balance and harmonic settings. The Egyptians used incense from aromatic woods to honor their gods with the belief that the smoke would rise into the heavens carrying their well wishes. In France, Doctor Jean Valnet used aromatherapy to treat illnesses, gangrene, and battle wounds. Jean Valnet wrote the book *Practice of Aromatherapy*, placing this practice on the map with an important piece of literature.

In a study by the department of nursing at Geochang Provincial College, the effects of the inhalation method using essential oils on blood pressure and stress responses of clients with essential hypertension were measured. The results found were the blood pressure, pulse, subjective stress, state anxiety, and serum cortisol levels among the three groups were significantly statistically different. This concludes that the inhalation method using essential oils can be considered an effective nursing intervention that reduces psychological stress responses and serum cortisol levels, as well as the blood pressure of clients with essential hypertension (Hwang 2006).

The information above was added to augment biofeedback, allowing the client to expand the effects of aroma sensitivity to the training in biofeedback. Heart Rate Variability Biofeedback is a technique that is useful in reducing stress and depression. When biofeedback is coupled with aromatherapy, the self-report of the client brings a greater reduction of anxiety and an increased state of happiness. Since the olfactory system is primitive, even more primitive than drugs, this is a useful technique to use in the addiction setting. When a strong aroma is smelled by the client, there is an immediate disruption in the neurological connections that causes instantaneous change that goes past the cortex into the core brain areas.

This observation supports Brain Plasticity Principle II, in the way that neurological bundles are changed by experience in this case disruption. In our neuroplasticity sessions, the client will come in and choose from a wide variety of smells (from peppermint, eucalyptus, and lavender to coconut lime). The client dabs the essential oil on a pulse point and is instructed to smell the aroma when they achieve a deep state of relaxation or high coherence (indicated as a green light with the EmWave biofeedback device). The client is instructed to follow the pacer on the biofeedback device with their abdominal breathing along with their choice of essential oil smell activating memories of relaxation. After a thirty-minute period of biofeedback training, the client reports their relaxation level and state of being. For time after the session, clients report that the simple whiff of the smell of their essential oil used during their training brings them back into relaxation immediately. Not only does this technique bring the client a deeper state of relaxation, it also gets them more engaged in their abdominal breathing process which is crucial in many aspects of life and well-being.

CD#2 Unity and Joy

This is the same CD described in an earlier chapter that was created by drumming at a frequency of 60 hertz for twenty-two minutes. What is assumed to be taking place in the brain is that the cingulate gyrus is not integrating the brain's different functions well; the metaphor is how an orchestra sounds when there is no director. The violins are playing at one tempo, the trombones are playing another, the percussion sections another, and so on. The entrainment of CD#2 (MindBodySeries) serves as the conductor and the selected frequency of 60 Hz. sets the tempo at approximately the low beta range. Repeated sessions in being exposed to this CD will eventually set a pattern for continued functioning in which the brain will stabilize and the obsession will disappear.

It should be noted that CD#2 can be used during other activities, such as driving and work; however, television waves often contradict the entrainment. The more it can be used during activities the more effective it can be.

Rhythmic Exercise

What Pat did adopt immediately was a daily regimen of dance and rhythmic music. When the body moves in a consistent movement, every organ and muscle will be impacted in the body, and if done consistently, an integration of muscular coordination will be built. This habitual integration is what happens when a person learns to play golf, tennis, or sports in general. Some call it "muscle memory."

The basic reason humans have that ability to reshape their bodies is because their brains are plastic enough to change nerve pathways very efficiently. Although this process affects the whole brain, a lot of credit goes to the cerebellum in the brain because it's responsible for the bundling of nerves and for coordinating them. It achieves this process by interacting with all of the brain, much like the cingulate gyrus does. It makes sense that if you stimulate the brain overall into rhythmic and harmonious connections, and the cingulated gyrus in particular, that the deregulation would be helped back to normal, naturally.

Rehearsal

The idea of rehearsals is to prepare for a performance. Success with
the practice of alternate methods for dealing with anxiety or fear can be
achieved through practice. The initiation of rehearsals begins with a deep
sense of relaxation which is achieved beforehand. Through the processes
in the patient's imagination, along with the addition of actionable methods of reassurance, the patient imagines or actually goes through a time
period in which the triggers are present and the usual emotional reactions take place, but in the presence of the relaxation and lower arousal
level the associations do not take place. It is more powerful if an influen-
tial music or rhythm is taking place so as to monitor the brain's rhythm.
A group of people can only hum, pray, chant for the same intention and
group imagery can be added for powerful rituals.

Breathing

Some impressive brain scans support the conclusion that "alternate
nostril breathing" (a specific breathing tool) has strong therapeutic value.
The patient exchanges alternate nostril breaths. Just gently press the index finger against the right nostril, so that it is blocked. Cycle through
slowly, purposefully, inhaling and exhaling through the left nostril; then,
switch nostrils. Continue until the patient feels a sense of calm. Then, do
it for six more minutes; which will equal three minutes per side. Brain
scans (QEEG) confirm a rapid change in frequency intensity.

Patients have successfully used this nostril breathing technique to halt
intrusive, obsessive thoughts; and it's a fine method even for the comforting aspect alone. Plus, new associations can be formed for a new inventory of anxiety-reducing practices.

Chanting

Just as the brain responds to music and rhythm, the impact is magnified when it responds to the internal vibrations made by our own vocal
chords. Chanting in repetition has been shown to shift the overall frequency toward alpha (which is the relaxation range), and tends to create
a harmonious level across the brain. The psychological impact is one of
feeling peaceful and confident.

The brain is designed to do what is verbally said as intention and
chanting a message will actually build neurons around suggestions. This
is most evident in sports psychology. As auditory messages are practiced,
the brain begins to create behavioral sequences and advances in sports
performances happen and this process is applicable to any and all goals.
The process is not without its requirements. It doesn't work to just say it
one time and everything goes in motion. Imagine that for every time a

chant or message is spoken, it grows one neuron connection. It is recommended repeating an intentional message 1,000 times a day.

Start by having the client choose one phrase, such as "I can do this" or "I am enough" to use as a chanting or mantra phrase. Spiritual ones, like "God loves me," "I am forgiven," and "God walks with me" have shown excellent results, as well. In the typical therapeutic interactions, the patient chooses specific phrases that pertain to a person's unique needs and brain function.

When a new brain pattern is formulated, the pattern has to integrate emotions and correct intentions. This goes with the advice of a great piano master about how he reached the heights he has, and he voiced this principle as his "secret" of success. He explained that if someone wants to be a piano player, they have to start with one note and understand the feeling and frequency of that note. Then, add another note and compare them. As they add the full complement of notes, they pay full attention and set their brain to each attunement. He also made a point of emphasizing that this doesn't just happen over the course of one day or in a year. His investment of thirty years attests to this discipline.

Neurotherapy

Neurotherapy is probably the most direct method for learning how to change the brain stress because the goals are precisely fixed for those reasons. If part of the brain, such as the cingulated gyrus, is overactive with high beta frequencies or is super low with delta frequencies and causing disruption, the process of neurotherapy would be to hook up an EEG monitor and attach electrodes primarily to the skin surface that measures the electromagnetic energy of that region, which would likely show the same extra-high levels as found on the QEEG brain scan (Hammond 2003).

The therapeutic process would involve the patient being educated as to the significance of the graphs generated on the computer monitor, including becoming knowledgeable as to what the dysfunctional ranges are, and utilizing the auditory and visual feedback. The EEG monitor serves like an emotional mirror; and with the help of a trained therapist, the patient can learn ways of balancing the discordant frequencies.

One of the patients displayed brain waves in the cingulated gyrus region that were really high and her emotional state was as if she was on a rollercoaster of ever-repeating images, much like PTSD. As she watched the monitor and heard some auditory feedback in the form of high and low tones, she discovered that the imagery of water created a positive change in the measurements. Later she learned that breathing patterns also helped in her control. Finally, she was able to lower these destructive, anxiety frequencies and replace them with slower but higher quality waveforms by imagining the wave forms themselves. Her concentration abilities improved practically immediately, and her emotional feelings of panic soon subsided.

Symbolic Imagery

The client will actually be using his or her brain's own internal mechanisms for help. Instead of only seeing the brain as weak and in chaos, they will also associate their brain as having the power of healing them as well. It takes about twenty-one days of consistent imagery to stabilize the association. Thus, if the client can stick with this imagery process for a mere twenty-one days the brain will incorporate the imagery within the storm neural network and have an internal key conflict resolution. In other words, the path to positive healing may only be twenty-one days away.

As an aside, embracing imagery as a tool for success isn't some wild, new-fangled idea: superstars, like Tony Dorsett of the Dallas Cowboys, have shared that he imagines himself like a running tornado—and few would argue that his spinning motion didn't have a great impact on his successful avoidance of being tackled. And of course you know that Olympic athletes are taught to visualize their events with success before their participation. There has even been research that suggests that imagery can improve not only coordination, but also strength (Murphy and White 1978).

Mindful Meditation

Living in the present moment is an impactful and powerful discipline that takes persistence. A group of researchers studied the effects of mindful meditation on cognitive processes and affect in patients with past depression. Their finding was consistent with this belief and the results suggest that "[m]indful meditation practice primarily leads to decreases in ruminative thinking, even after controlling for reductions in affective symptoms and dysfunctional beliefs" (Ramel, Goldin, Carmona, and McQuaid 2004).

Pat was able to practice mindful meditation techniques, and has been able to jump the hurdle of hearing destructive voices from the past and able to prune her brain to disallow thoughts about her stepfather and the horrifying turn of events. There are various exercises that clients can practice that direct the brain to stay in the present moment. These exercises are simple and easy to follow such as using your non-dominant hand so that you can pay extra attention to any task that you are tending to. Just about anything can be used to implement mindful meditation and assisting the patient to encounter their own ways to practice can be most productive. Pat found and learned mindful meditation exercises quickly and kept a journal of the lessons learned from practicing these techniques.

OVERALL THOUGHTS

The ruminating, obsessive brain is perhaps the most destructive of all stress storms because it's so incapacitating to the individual. The patient feels trapped in their own private hell of which they feel there is no escape. The process toward addiction occurs when the patient realizes they are behaving in bizarre and strange ways and obsessing in ritualistic behavior, but they feel powerless, and too afraid to change. The fear is unbearable; although in their minds they know it's not reality. They can't make sense of why they behave as if someone else was controlling them. Drugs offer an answer; however, they come with a high price—temporary relief in exchange for profound depths of confusion and depression, anxiety, and turmoil for the rest of their lives.

The exciting thing is that there is hope. There are some controls the client can find in rhythmic movement, neurotherapy, nutrition, and a host of personal changes they can incorporate into their daily life to control the brain and banish this drug-induced hell from their reality, and it's time now for them to step into a better and joyous life. The brain can be reset with the right tools. The sense of true self, real choice, and freedom will emerge.

TEN

Multi-Polar or Rage Barriers

The stories are usually the same—the "mean alcoholic" goes through a transition from Dr. Jekyll to Mr. Hyde and destroys family relationships, property, and anything and everything in their path. In many instances, this transition does not occur just because of substance abuse. There is a rage factor that can be activated in seconds even when sober. Known in psychiatric circles as the "bipolar disorder," a.k.a. "manic-depressive," the syndrome is a range of moods from euphoria to deep depression with cycles that last anywhere from minutes to days.

JOHN'S STORY

Already a common story in the mental health system (and to the judicial system), John appeared far older than his twenty-eight years on the planet would suggest. He looked to most as a downtrodden, beaten man. His eyes were dark and weary, his face was deeply lined and sagging, and no matter whether he was sitting, standing, or walking, his shoulders remained hunched over. Between his stays at rehab facilities and his extensive time in jail, he'd spent more than half his life in institutions.

John's experiences in addiction programs usually followed the same script. He would be given the choices of rehab or jail time and depending on exact mood at the time he would choose either, but his performances in rehab always ended with some rage in which he would damage some property, scare the hell out of the staff, and which ultimately would end in his discharge.

His primary mental health issue was depression resulting in suicidal ideation, and the scars on his wrists testified to the depths of his desperation. In terms of his recidivism in the judicial system, his most egregious behavior was kidnapping; he'd taken a teenager across state lines, in an attempt to extract ransom money from the teen's parents. Some of his "lesser" crimes (that also landed him in jail) included writing bad checks, identity theft, and illegal gambling. He described each of these events as a giving him a "fabulous high" —one in which he felt fearless, invincible, and incredibly energized. In fact, he characterized the overall feeling as exhilarating.

Understanding John's family history and upbringing didn't provide any clues. His parents were both teachers and the stories he'd shared about their parenting sounded fairly traditional. There was little trauma in his rural Michigan setting that would indicate childhood issues, for example, there were no gangs, no catastrophic events, and so on.

John married early at the age of nineteen to a young woman who he described as "silly." Although the way he described her behavior during their conflicts made everyone laugh, to his clinicians it was alarming. For example, he told of explosive, angry outbursts over "issues" of contention where she'd throw pots, pans, skillets, hammers, and even kitchen cutlery and would follow his tales by displaying his scars as proof. Interestingly, when asked what the issues were, he could never remember. Their marriage ended after six months. He'd made that choice after awakening from being in a coma for seven days, the result of a direct hit to his head with an iron skillet she'd catapulted from across the room.

Four years later, he gave marriage another try with a different woman. This time he admitted responsibility for the problems (and ultimately its break-up), and for the first time, he remembered the onset of his own chaotic behavioral changes. As if for no reason, suddenly he'd start gambling away his weekly paycheck, and of course lied about doing so. He would go on frenzied shopping sprees (on somebody else's stolen credit card), bringing home to his wife odd gifts she never wanted like a super expensive bicycle, a painting of a nude person, and even a set of mechanic tools.

Then, like shattering the bottom out of an hourglass, his hyper-energy abruptly drained out of him. Sinking ever lower into a hole of despondency, his mood now shifted from all-knowing all-powerful omniscience to being that of an overly obedient child, deferring to anyone's thoughts or judgments over his own. He was profoundly out of control, and his wife had him hospitalized. Soon thereafter, she'd had enough and left him.

As predicted, he was diagnosed with bipolar disorder. He was prescribed two medications that brought him substantial relief. One was lithium, which is a type of mineral salt (and one of the primordial elements) that functions very well as a mood stabilizer; the other medication was an anti-depressant. When he arrived at my clinic, he was rational, clearly under control, and there was a mutual agreement that there was still hope for him.

When John's SPECT-Scan was cleared, the story made perfect sense so an immediate plan of action was made. The scan had revealed a "multi-polar stress pattern"—which looks like a gas stove burner with hot edges around the brain, affecting the prefrontal areas deep into the temporal regions. This storm is similar to the anxiety storm, but it's far, far more intense. Even John's "relaxed" state was intense. His muscle tension was physically visible, especially in his neck. His blood pressure varied to the extremes, rising way above and way below the charts, with little in between. It was not clear if John even knew what normal felt like, as his brain storm energy levels were so intense.

Redefining His Life

John's brain state was consistent with the consequences of the head trauma incurred from his first wife's antics, which might have related to a mixture of brain injury coupled with the high stress situation. To jump ahead to the final steps of his follow-up, John found several things that helped his life. He discovered that practicing breathing techniques gave him a sense of balance. As you may recall, this activity helps control the heart-rate variability, and in his experience, it also checked his erratic hormonal pattern as well. Exhibiting great discipline and ongoing commitment, he practiced these breathing exercises at least three times a day. In fact, he became so good at it, that it became a tool he could count on (which is the goal). For example, anytime he noted a rise in his emotional intensity, even if it were positive, he would use the breathing technique he had learned to stabilize his state. That way he could actually enjoy the excitement while being relaxed.

As his mastery grew, he raised the bar and started using imagery as part of his breathing exercises. For example, he would visualize beautiful, golden-rose colored "love smoke" swirling gently into his heart to bring his heart-rate variability into balance—which also made him feel better about himself and his abilities to take control of his life. Light now replaced the weary look in his eyes, which I dare say sparkled when he would describe his latest calming and empowering visuals. John also briefly used BAUD-assisted neurotherapy to help him lower the anxiety and stress in his brain. Once he found a frequency that gave him relief, he was satisfied that he had backup.

After some time, John joined a religious sect that meditated most of the day, wore robes, and released all possessions but the barest of essentials for warmth. He embraced the spiritual dogma of love for himself and others, in which he found a profound sense of peace. With the glow in his eyes and the flowing robe, he reminded me of a monk without the bald head.

The Multi-Polar Brain Pattern

The multi-polar stress pattern suggests the deepest onset of anxiety one could imagine in the temporal lobes (which are responsive to emotional stability). The brain appears inflamed with over-stimulating excitement in multiple directions. Depressive events may shift to the outer limits of pain. And frankly, any emotional response could trigger a perilous challenge; even jubilation could be turned into a frenzied state, which could explain the pull toward risky.

The strategies for disarming this alarm system have to be complex, and it takes enormous concentration and discipline to learn to control the high arousals. There is a clear similarity between the protocols for anxiety and multimodal complex because they are both of high intensity; however, the high reactivity of the multimodal is likely caused by the high levels of brain inflammation. In John's case, since he was using alcohol for many years his brain was already inflamed from the abuse. There are several other triggers of inflammatory issues:

1. allergies to food, pesticides
2. food sensitivities to sugar, wheat, lactose
3. perfumes

In order to rule in what kinds of environmental factors that could be causing inflammatory onsets, a food diary is offered in Appendix B.

PROTOCOLS

A person may not want to go the same route as John, as he conquered his demons by adopting an intense spiritual discipline; although the important factor is that a decision was made to change his life. That in and of itself may be what ultimately worked for him, in the same way the Twelve Steps have helped others through their own transformations. While there absolutely are medications that can be profoundly helpful, just taking a pill, without doing the emotional and spiritual work, is rarely a long-term solution.

The goals of any remedy starts with a commitment to making a difference from within. With addiction, it starts with understanding complete hopelessness that provides willingness to make this commitment. Doing so cues your brain that you're about to start a new life path. This takes courage because not everything you think, do, or try is going to work, but there will be answers and most likely many of them. You don't have to live with this storm because you have the potential and the capacity to win this war. Thinking otherwise is your storm deceiving you. Based on the five principles of brain plasticity, described below are some avenues I recommend you consider to help you take back control in order for someone to start working a program of recovery.

BAUD

Like the protocol of anxiety control, the BAUD is used to help the person gain control of the storms of high beta waves, and hence anxiety, when he feels rage begin to fill his mind. The steps are clear for the first time and it would be great but not critical to monitor the brain rhythms to document that control is validated. The patient's sense of relaxation can be enough. Have the patient adjust the upper right knob (frequency/ pitch) until some sense of relaxation or peace is felt. Then increase the sensation with the upper left knob. The volumes on both ears should be loud enough to detract the brain toward the sounds.

Once the knobs have been set for successful calming, begin to do breathing cycling that helps the relaxation process as well. Continue until the patient feels that he or she has control.

Josh grew up in a house of perfectionist values spearheaded by his father. As a child, Josh remembered watching his father as he entered fitness competitions, ate nothing but clean food, and kept the house in an orderly fashion. Josh, like any child, went through a rebellion phase and this included eating a sugar-filled diet and not attending the weekly training sessions his father had put in place for him. Josh ended up packing on serious pounds and later left his home due to the trauma incurred from the never-ceasing ruthlessness from his father. When Josh came to the treatment center, he was full of hate and rage. I can still picture the day he came in—collared shirt, red faced, and sitting at the back of the cafeteria not talking to anyone. At this point in his life, Josh dropped all the heavy pounds and he too was a body builder like his father. Josh came into his first PNP session and admitted he struggled with extreme feelings of rage on a daily basis that were only satisfied by hitting the gym. Josh accomplished breath training and once he got the hang of it, he noticed it helped significantly, but it was the BAUD device that helped him the most. Josh placed the headphones on with a curiosity as to whether this sonic stimulation would actually work for him. After choosing his relaxation setting, Josh said he felt as if he went to another world. While deep breathing with the sound, Josh said he imagined himself under a tree on a blanket feeling deeply relaxed. From this point forward, it was easier for Josh to connect into the recovery program and his community since he no longer became flustered from any insignificant occurrence.

Note: If the trigger to the rage is food sensitivity, the sounds may be irritating and an alternative approach should be advised. This is often the case of autistic patients who are very sensory irritated. Option: see Entrainment using CDs.

Neurotherapy

If there's anything that one can bet on, it's that the brain is always learning and it is a choice on what to teach it. There are professional ways of fine-tuning the brain to change into more normal patterns and the science and art of this process is through a form of therapy called "neuro-therapy," a cornerstone for brain change. This approach has been mentioned in earlier chapters, so hopefully it is beginning to feel familiar with its concepts. In the case of the multi-polar brain storm, the main idea is to calm the brain and lower the intensity around the temporal and frontal lobes. The protocol is pretty straightforward: electrode receptors are placed on your head above these areas and verify the high levels of Beta and even Gamma (the next highest levels). As a person watches the computer monitor to see their high levels being pictured as lines marching across the screen as they change or there are even games he or she can play that are converted. For example, the individual might play basketball or match points as he or she starts teaching the brain to come under their control.

Like learning to wiggle ears by looking in a mirror, the individual finds ways to teach the brain to become less sensitive and more focused. It takes about fifty sessions to really learn this well.

Hyperbaric Chamber

For those unfamiliar with the hyperbaric chamber, this pressured chamber was originally built for ocean divers who came to the surface too quickly and developed the bends. When placed back in the pressure with oxygen-enriched air in which they were diving and gradually

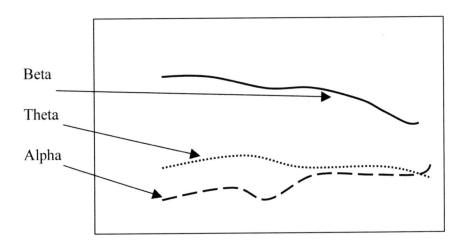

Figure 10.1.   Relative Comparison to Brain Dynamics

brought to surface pressure, they were cured of the near disastrous problem. A similar protocol has been used to hasten wound and brain healing by exposing the patient to a "dive" of approximately an hour in which they are exposed to an oxygen enriched pressure of 1.5 atmospheres (approximately 1.5 the air pressure at the surface). Research studies signal that the hyperbaric chamber also decreases neuro-inflammation of rats with traumatic brain injury (Vlodavsky, Palzur, and Soustiel 2006).

As examined from a brain model, one of the side effects of an inflamed brain is high irritation, anxiety, and rage. This is often called the "hot brain" syndrome related to PTSD affected brains. One of the most impressive outcomes of exposing a patient who has been full of rage and anger beyond reason for circumstances is a welcome resolution to the impulsive reactions. It is suggested that a person be exposed to twenty 1-hour sessions or fifteen 90-minute sessions.

Rhythmic Physical Exercise

Rhythmic exercise has great benefit for resolving the multi-polar brain pattern. However, be sure to choose gentle, slow, relaxing exercise, such as Tai' Chi or Yoga. The slow process of exercise appears to hasten the relaxation and harmonizing processes. Too often, the people with this brain pattern tend to want to move in accordance to their high brain energy. It's vital for success to allow the brain the opportunity to follow the soothing process of the muscular system. The importance of this physical influence cannot be overemphasized. Indeed, the pace itself is an important component. For example, when one walks very quickly, the brain follows suit. The need is to do the reverse. This takes practice for someone in the multi-polar brain pattern. But it can be done.

When Frank was thirteen years old he went out for football, a sport he craved to play, but he was a very, very slow runner. In wind sprints, he would usually meet the group running back and turn around at midstream. The reason he was so slow was that he held his breath while he was running, though he didn't know he was doing this. Frank became stressed and eventually lost his motivation to even try. It wasn't until he went out for cross-country running (with the encouragement of his coach) that he discovered the benefits of coordinating breathing and running. He soon became one of the fastest players, even into college levels. This is the concept he needed to embrace—learning to relax and breathe while doing what is desired.

Entrainment by Listening to Relaxation CDs

Similar to the chanting, listening to relaxation CD instructions (such as those from the MindBodySeries website), can develop shifts in the brain while simply listening. They also have the added benefit of becoming associated with the instructions automatically. Listening to a CD is recommended—at least fifty times—creating a brain neuro-network of its own. By the fifth time in listening, the brain would have probably memorized the content and by the tenth time the brain would likely be anticipating the steps. By the fiftieth time, it would become automatic.

The brain mechanism might be imagined, how it creates relaxation repeatedly, with the words becoming memorized and integrated as the neurons begin to make new connections and positive associations to the words. Some people focus on what is particularly relaxing when listening to certain sections of the music, so one can even just listen to that portion. As the networks get broader and habit-strength gets built, the brain may eventually start the relaxation process simply by the individual touching the start button on the CD player. Pretty soon, all the individual has to do is imagine touching the machine and the relaxing process will become engaged. Once a person has gone through these steps to the point where the brain thoroughly integrates this association (Principle I of neuroplasticity), the brain will have learned how to relax through association.

Slow Practice by Rehearsal

By far the best way to eliminate the anxiety patterns and learn to focus is by success. And how to make sure there is success is to practice success by imagining it. This is called *mental rehearsal* and has been used by the armed forces for generations in their preparation for the anxiety of war. Somewhat similar in concept, what the military discovered long ago was that it is generally not human nature to want to kill each other. Therefore, soldiers are trained to not hesitate in their actions by having them practice creating the imagery of doing so in their minds. Needless to say, actually killing people to desensitize the soldiers in the training process is not an option, and reliance on pure imagery is sufficient.

Likewise, mental rehearsal imagery can work. In the mind, extinguish the emotional response to triggers with breathing or other techniques, and instead focus upon the reshaping of your responses toward a more constructive one. Carry out the total behavior as visualized as success in managing this overwhelming emotional powder barrel. If the brain is inflamed with toxicity, this process may be more difficult, but if one continues to process the imagery slowly, imagining with every breath, every movement, what it will smell like, what it will feel like, the brain will respond to the experience, especially if it is positively rewarded.

Mark had a story very similar to John's life. Mark had these moments of feeling out of control, especially when it came to his wife and their heated arguments. When Mark came into treatment, he dealt with the very high highs and the extremely low lows. After working a rigorous PNP program, Mark came to a point where he needed to practice all that he had learned through imagery. Mark was taken through different scenarios and felt the emotional responses he had with each step of the imagery. Mark's physiological response was apparent when he was going through a scenario that caused anger, his heart rate jumping at least twenty beats per minute and the return of sweaty palms. Mark would be instructed to breathe deeply and practice all the relaxation stress signal cues he had learned. Eventually with a lot of practice, Mark was able to go through the mental rehearsal on his own and even cue himself to use relaxation techniques.

It may be very useful to have a coach or even create a personal CD with the steps desired so the individual does not have to remember all of them. Repeat these exercises over a hundred times in order to replace the neuro networks you want to replace.

Chewing Gum

From the brain scan studies, the chewing action appears to pump blood into the temporal and part of the frontal lobe, making one feel less stressed and increase memories. It is usually recommended that those gum products that are suggested by the American Dental Association, making the act healthier for your teeth as well.

Note: Please see chapter 6 for more information on the benefits of chewing gum.

Biofeedback

Biofeedback is a more general method of learning to calm the brain. Many times the brain activity is reflected in body functions, such as higher blood pressure, restricted blood flow in your extremities, and muscle tension. Through the practice of learning to relax these processes, the patient will learn to calm his or her whole body.

By training the body to function with less stress and more efficiency, the brain will literally have an increased ability to think more clearly and

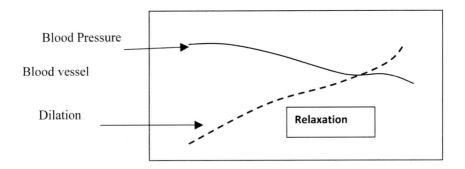

Figure 10.2. Biofeedback Dynamics

will be able to respond in ways that are appropriate and proportionate. To help optimize success, many people find it helpful to first go through a couple of training sessions with a certified biofeedback therapist to be reassured they are on the right path.

Brenda carried a web of complications around with her, not only did she have legal problems because of her drug use but she also was close to losing her kids forever because of her record and an ugly court case with her ex-husband. Brenda came to the treatment center fully guarded with anger burning behind her eyes. The community would stay away from her for fear of what she would say to them, and she looked as if she was ready to burst. Brenda needed relief. Every part of her body was tense, even her posture seemed as if she was in constant vigilance. At first, Brenda was not much of a talker and so on our first session she did little talking and more action. Brenda learned how to use her breath as her vehicle to self-calm. Some of the arousal tension melted away from her body during her first training. Brenda came back the next day and inquired if she could use the device again. Brenda found a way to relieve all of the anger she was holding in her body for so long and found something other than the booze to soothe this. Eventually, she came to find out that this type of biofeedback training was miles better than the alcohol because it had a lasting positive affect and would be an opening to a higher power that she still cherishes to this day. This was the higher power that she says restored her to sanity.

Breathing: The Ancient Process

Various breathing techniques have been in use since the beginning of recorded history. In the case of the multi-polar brain storm, the pattern of breathing that has been proven to be of enormous help is the combination of two configurations: (1) the alternative nostril breathing protocol, and (2) the box breathing protocol. Box breathing (4-count inhale, 4-count hold, 4-count exhale, and 4-count hold; repeat)—this method is often used in a therapeutic situation for resolution of anxiety. For example, if a person is dealing with fear of heights or having some panic about dying, this would be an appropriate method to try. All emotions can be controlled and diminished through this method. That is exactly what one wants to accomplish for the multi-polar brain storm.

Box breathing is based on a "square" formula of 4-4-4-4 counts, meaning the person breathes in for a count of four, (1-2-3-4), holds it for a count of four (1-2-3-4), exhales to the count of four (1-2-3-4), and then waits to breathe in for a count of four (1-2-3-4). It is the last effort of not breathing in that often brings up the fear.

The QEEG brain maps usually register a shift to balanced frequencies across the brain regions, especially in the frontal and temporal lobe areas where activity is so high. For many of us, our ultimate fear is the fear of death or being exiled and/or becoming nothing. As an individual goes through these cycles, he or she will probably note that although the phases are all four-count, there may nonetheless be the sense of anxiety about getting enough air. It is the distrust in the procedure, or the world, that is the implied association; therefore, the brain fears the possible lack of air as the person refuses to breathe in for a 4-count. In a way of thinking about excitement in the brain, the sources of fear often emerge in your imagination or fantasies. Consciously take the leap of faith that holding the breath for a 4-count won't result in death and the brain will quickly catch on to the reality of the situation and to the success.

Chanting and Mantras

As discussed in Principle I, chanting the same word or words repeatedly has been very helpful for providing relief from the multi-polar brain storm. By repeating the same phrase, the brain begins to form networks around the verbal expression and eventually around the positive message. In so doing, since the brain can only handle so much processing (and brain cells have a way of jumping ship from less-used functions to more-used functions), this type of focused thinking can set the brain up to broadcast the messages wanted and delete the ones that serve us poorly.

The brain listens to the internal dialogue that people say to themselves, and basically, if someone talks in one message long enough, it will crowd the others out. For example, if John's usual internal messages are based on fear and anxiety, such as "You are going to be afraid, you are going to fail, you are going to lose control," John's brain is going to be set on high alert and look for the signal. If he repeats words of comfort and strength, such as "I am enough, I can handle this, I will be OK," these phrases will become dominant and ease out the negative ones.

Corbin was a client that went very far in his progression during his time in the facility. He started off as a mad, irritable, and perturbed man that wanted so badly to leave treatment and tend to his marijuana farm. He would repeat to himself that marijuana would be the only thing in the world that would calm him down. He was wrong. After many PNP sessions and many hours of practice, Corbin started to embrace his spiritual practice of meditation. And although he did not admit it at first, and liked to play the "tough guy" card, he eventually confessed that meditation was one of the best things he had found that allowed him to connect to his inner self and heart. Even though it was wonderful and Corbin found an inspiring practice, he still struggled with feeling self-assured. He felt like he was a failure for being in treatment and did not think very highly of himself and worried about his lack of successes. Corbin was encouraged to make up a mantra that he could repeat to himself to build a self-confidence brain track. Corbin smiled brightly once he realized his mantra of "I can be that kind of man." He explained that even as a child he always had a picture in mind of the man he wanted to become one day. He never knew this was a possibility until now. To this day, Corbin still tells himself his mantra before every meditation. His self-esteem has grown, and he has become a strong influence in the recovery community. He now runs a sober house and has taken pride in the work he is doing in the world.

Reach for a Team

Finding a team is very helpful to gain brain support toward better confidence for the multi-polar brain pattern. Multiple brain cycles can create a mutual effort to override the cycle, but it's important to choose three distinct personality types: a coach, a peer, and a supporter. The coach person is the one who focuses on training of successful habits and insists on the correct behavior. This is a person who has a plan and serves as a teacher and the patient follows his or her guidance without question. The peer person is an individual who's a friend and works as a partner. Both parties have similar goals, so both are participants as well as partners and work together in supporting each other. The supportive person is the individual who celebrates every effort and reviews advancements in any way feasible with social rewards.

Sleep CD

The restorative powers of sleep cannot be overstated. Sleep is critically necessary for the brain to successfully readjust and organize its experiences; nerve bundles are formed, reshaped, and rerouted. If the patient is one of those people who says, "I'll sleep when I'm dead" it might be true. In other words, getting a minimum of eight to nine hours sleep is not "optional." It's essential to mental health. If the laundry does not get done as fast as desired, or the house remains a bit cluttered, so be it.

Celebrate Each Step

This sounds redundant to the other programs, and the reason is that this step must be done to stabilize the desired changes in the brain. This can be termed positive reinforcement. It should be done for every step, regardless of how small, toward the desired mental state. It can include any form of support one can create, including social ("Atta boys," pats on the back, hugs, trophies, etc.), physical (good food, rest, vacations, etc.), psychological (awards, recognition, parking spaces, etc.), or any emotional currency that found to be successful.

It is important to remember that one has control over all that is done, and one of the options that one has is changing the brain, not matter how "late" one thinks it is or where one is. Even in prison there is always the option of how to perceive the situation and what to do about it. If one engages in these protocols one can build new healthy brain tracks. Change the neural brain tracks, change one's life.

ELEVEN

Brain Plasticity and Spirituality

It may sound strange to consider the science of neurology in conjunction with the philosophical aspects of spirituality; however, there is a wonderful connection between the two. The basis of all religions comes down to one central agreement: there exists an essential part of humankind that contains the awareness of infinite immortality and that life exists beyond our perceptions of what is directly experienced. There is an inner wisdom that exists within each of us which can provide the direct path toward our true destinies. That inner wisdom is both within our brain and outside us in the sense of personal knowledge and worldly control.

It is a basic necessity in our individual quest for peace and order to find a congruency between our sense of self and this highest inner wisdom. Making this connection and finding some avenue of communication is a significant requisite in order to live our lives accordingly.

When an addict comes into treatment, not only is it a goal for them to detox from the substance they have been abusing, but also to rewire their brain to perceive an entity greater than themselves and thus renew their life trajectory. Spirituality has been incredibly beneficial in the progress of health, especially with addicts. The stories have been heard of patients lying on their death bed who had such a deep faith in some higher power beyond themselves that they were able to combat their illness successfully and regain their life. For the transformation of sobriety to occur within the prescriptions of the Twelve Steps, this initial awareness of a Higher Power appears to be affirmed and the awareness of the great resources found through this discovery is a critical element of recovery. Otherwise, any steps worked are still based on self-serving needs being met with only a minimum of power sought for moving beyond the status quo both psychologically and physically.

WHAT IS SPIRITUALITY?

Spirituality is a concept that holds many views, opinions and models. In the dictionary, spirit is defined as "the principle of conscious life; the vital principle in humans, animating the body or mediating between body and soul" (Dictionary.com 2014). To a Buddhist, this state of being would be called the "Buddha nature," which is the sacred nature required to be a Buddha in the world. The sacred nature is a realization that all beings have the same potential and nature to gain enlightenment. To a Christian, spirituality would mean the journey to find "self" through one's relationship with God. To each individual the idea of spirituality is unique to their state of being and personal belief system. However; there seems to be a correlation with how the brain responds to spirituality which is where neuroplasticity plays a significant role. In a study done with the University of Pennsylvania, they found that a Buddhist monk meditating and a Franciscan nun going into centered prayer have similar localized neural activity (measured with a SPECT scan) in the same area of the brain (Newberg and d'Aquili 2008). Since the brain reacts to the different types of spiritualties the same, there is potential that no matter what one's belief, there is a positive outcome within the brain and thus every cell in the physical body. This is especially significant for addicts working the Twelve Steps. In Step Two of the Twelve Steps of AA, there must be something larger than the addict that is believed in, which will restore them to sanity. The Big Book does not signify what type of spirituality, as long as there is a higher power that the addict or alcoholic could surrender to. Spirituality allows the addict to make new neuro-pathways within the brain and neuroplasticity reveals that the brain is the instrument of this change, based on experience and training. If you spend your life journey helping others and integrating a higher power into your everyday life, your neural networks within your brain will certainly reflect this. In short, changing your life will change your brain and changing your brain will change your life. One of the most profoundly significant ways to change your life is through spirit which comes from the Latin word "spiritus," which means breath.

MONA

Mona was a true heroin addict whose addiction undermined her life goals and provided a strong barrier from her spiritual awareness. As she approached the rehab facility on her twenty-first birthday she was angry and determined to return to the only way of happiness she had ever found: drugs. There was nothing that she was not willing to do to get the drugs that her mind and body demanded. Prostitution in exchange for drugs was the way of life she knew for over three years, and she knew how to seduce and manipulate to get her way with certain police officers in order to stay out of jail.

When Mona was first presented the Twelve Steps program, and her counselor brought up the concept of a "higher power," she laughed hysterically. "Are you talking about God? Are you f__king talking about God? He's a man, O.K.? And I f__k men. And the last thing I need in my life is another man to f__k me or tell me how to run my life. Do you know what men do to me? I say F___K them all!"

She raged for a long time before she finally became more internally focused, and explained, "I used to believe in God and tried to be what He wanted me to be. My parents were always telling me what a mess-up I was, and how God didn't like little girls who did what I did. I was always screwing up, breaking rules, saying bad things and disappointing this make-believe 'Santa Claus' fake man that kept telling me I was 'bad' inside. But I found out I was being lied to, and there is no way I will give my control to something that isn't real."

As Mona's brain began its slow detoxification, her rational brain began to lose some of the anger. She appeared to crave a diet of high good fats and low sugar as she felt better and more secure. A BAUD session disrupting some of the overlying anger emotions appeared to open another wall of resistance of depression. The past conflicts with her mother erupted into very intense feelings of shame and turmoil, which included deep feeling and beliefs of being a failure. A second BAUD session with the purpose of disrupting the depressive thoughts turned her mind toward self-identification and personal confusion of life goals. For approximately seven days she wandered around the facility with a look as if she had just been awakened to questions she should have answered many years back. Many talks with her counselors revealed new information, and she was excited about the possibilities of what the answers may be.

Mona asked to stay in the sensory deprivation chamber (SDC) so she could just be without distraction. Her first stay was thirty minutes and when she emerged there was a glow on her face that had never been seen before. In discussions, she reported that her mother suddenly appeared as real as day and they began to have long conversations that involved both of them forgiving each other. She was forgiven because she was not the easiest child during adolescence, and she forgave her mother for not being the best mother. When asked what age her mother was, she replied frankly that her mother had died three years ago. This experience showed a total renewal in her commitment to the discovery of a new transformed identity.

After several sessions in breathing and biofeedback, Mona was invited to attend a "vision quest" experience in which she might gain some new insight and perspective on her goals. The group was led into a deep relaxation phase and instructed to walk through a forest and when she had reached a "safe place" she was asked to sit or lie down and await something to appear. Almost at once she saw a deer stag with a wonderful set of antlers that reached into the sky. The deer had looked into Mona's eyes with a comforting stare that conveyed love. Somewhere in her mind she heard these words: "Be not afraid, for I am with you."

Mona could hardly hold her tears back as she described this experience and she eagerly wanted to understand why that had happened. In true shamanic form, the deer symbol was explained as the nurturing promise to humankind that the animal would serve as food, love, nurturance, and guidance for her life. It gave the promise that she would not only return to her in this way, but that spirit of the deer was always with her. Mona grasped the meaning immediately and became focused on her experience. She drew pictures of her stag, found pictures in magazines and stories of stag. She planned to have a tattoo of a stag over her heart. She experienced the vision quest several times and the stag was always there as her spiritual ally.

Finally she asked what the stag was on spiritual levels and the explanation was simply a symbol of God with a message for her. Being of a traditional religious background, this explanation was difficult to integrate with her original concepts, but she embraced herself as worthy of God's love because of this direct experience of her own. She could rely on this deep and profound experience rather than what someone told her or what she could read in a book. In this way, the experience is always there with her. So, in her step work, as she progressed to Step Two, she was more than willing to believe something greater than herself could restore her to sanity. Mona now knew that she had to choose her own conception of God and this was exactly what she integrated after her spiritual experience with the stag in her vision quest.

NEUROLOGY AND SPIRITUALITY

The connection between neurology and spirituality appears to be a natural consequence of reaching a specific brain state so that the person can receive spiritual understandings. This brain state can be created and achieved through various protocols and under certain conditions. One of those conditions often heard about is the "near-death experience" in which a person actually enters the death shut down and has a profound experience such as hearing angels, Jesus Christ, God, ancestors, or other beings on the spiritual plane, moving toward a white light, and being immersed in "love and compassion." The reports by people that have near-death experiences are almost identical in the messages conveyed, consisting of an ever present love on the other side.

There are also vivid visions and dreams that present themselves with messages specifically for the individual, such as burning bushes, major traumatic storms of powers, words of comfort, and others of a specific event to come.

There have been reports in history of rituals intentionally administered for the alteration of the state of consciousness in order to communicate in the field of spirituality, such as fasting, sleep deprivation, holotropic breathwork, sun dance rituals in which the individual is suspended by hooks driven through their pectoral muscles for some period of time in order to experience and overcome an overwhelmingly intense pain, and other means of extraordinary physical conditions. LSD was considered to be a major breakthrough by psychiatry for a short time to provide these elevations into the understandings of ourselves.

These rituals have the validity of providing shifts of consciousness but not necessarily spiritual consciousness. The elements of "spiritual connections" as described with other approaches do not offer the same richness and continued profound insights, especially those involving love and personal evolution.

Nevertheless, there have been and still are ministries that carry the missions of spiritual connections and have long and intensive training to achieve this specific mind set. These areas of training are best described in Buddhism and intense early Christian traditions (such as the Rosicrucians and Catholic monasteries).

Taken from the literature as a whole and reports of spiritual states, such as Mona's, there appears to be six direct natural connections from the brain dynamics and spiritual consciousness:

- A perceived place of personal and emotional safety
- Removal of the ego (personal control)
- Priority shift from selfish survival to altruistic motivations (Maslow)
- Brain state is dominated by slow alpha and theta wave forms
- The mind is active and open to symbolic forms of communication
- While the mind is active it is devoid of distractions of a personal fear-based motive.

While these constructs overlay each other, the pattern appears consistent that when the person has been taught or intentionally enters these six dimensions of brain metrics, there is an automatic exposure to the spiritual levels. But while it may be simple to express, it may be extraordinarily difficult to achieve these precise levels, especially if there is distracting demands and conflicts.

When PNP principles are focused on achieving a spiritual level, the brain parameters are pretty well determined.

- A perceived place of personal and emotional safety is determined by suggestions and training in finding a safe place in the imagination and practice in quickly equipping oneself with a situation of deep relaxation. This can be accomplished within a group or individually.

- Removal of the ego (personal control) can be accomplished by purposefully releasing ego control through suggestions, practice through the experience of safety and faith in the procedures of relaxation, and comfort through symbols.
- Priority shift from selfish survival to altruistic motivations can be accomplished through suggestion and experience with an accomplished therapist and imagery situations of self-arising over fear and instinctual motivations for self-control through BAUD disruptions of mythic beliefs.
- Brain state dominated by slow alpha and theta wave forms which can be achieved through biofeedback, time in the sensory deprivation chamber, mindful meditation, and breath training.
- The mind is active and open to the symbolic forms of communication that are parts of the vision quest, spirit animal meditations, and other rituals of self-empowerment.
- While the mind is active, it is devoid of distractions of a personal fear-based motive and results in resolutions of fear-based beliefs and thus helps in finding relaxation states and coping skills for anxiety or anger in face of provocative stimuli.

OBSTACLES TO SPIRITUAL RESOURCES

When the list of obstacles to spiritual resources is listed, the first will always be addiction itself because of the disruptive elements that poison the brain and dominate all its pleasure centers. Addiction cancels out all other resources of morality, spirituality, legality, pride, and loyalty. The brain cancels out any other choice of pleasure and sense of commitment or efforts toward any other goal other than to acquire and use the addicted substance. Until that toxic element is disposed of and detoxed out of the system, there is always the blockage to any other resource for self-development or happiness.

By far the most prominent among the challenges to experience a spiritual connection are the three primary poisons of life: greed, hatred, and delusion. These are forms of ego investment into self and thus selfishness rules. This is similar to the rules of survival in which a person always feels threatened to the loss or fear of insufficiency and therefore attempts to maintain control through intimidation and self-serving tactics. This is a person who cannot be peaceful for fear of losing face or possession. This is a form of obsessive anxiety. In Step Three of the Twelve Steps, selfishness and self-centeredness is the root of all troubles for the addicted person and this principle remains true for all of us. It also explains that in order to recover, selfishness has to be removed from the addict or the disease will eventually kill them. Of course, this must be accomplished through an entity bigger than themselves.

The third factor that is an obstacle to spiritual planes is most likely a form of depression that may pre-date addiction in its root form based on a lack of self-worth. If one does not honor one's self, how could the higher power honor the self? Sometimes these self-perceptions are more powerful in the way parents blame their children for unforgivable sins and their lack of respect that undermines a sense of safety and love, but the experience of addiction itself is a major factor in this blockage.

Another important barrier in achieving spiritual connection and faith is the lack of experience and ability to release control to other sources. Sometimes this takes the form of a fast brain that cannot slow down to ever experience peace, much less experience a safe place in the heart of emotions.

PROTOCOLS

Sensory Deprivation Chamber (SDC)

In 1954 John C. Lilly (1977) introduced an apparatus in which the subject would not be distracted by touch, sound or light. The device was basically a soundproof tent over a tub that was filled with salt water to support a human body in suspension and served as an environment where the mind could be relieved of all environmental "noise" and focus on relevancy of the brain (whatever happened there was much excitement around this topic of consciousness, in the same era of LSD, and all the reports were positive in nature).

The PNP sensory deprivation chamber (SDC) was designed and built with similar intentions; however, several limitations had to be redesigned in order to fit the needs of the patients. Namely, the salt water was very difficult to manage for sanitary reasons, comfort of patients, maintenance of floor conditions, and temperature control so the salt does not crystallize, to name a few.

In the SDC at the PNP center, a heated water mattress to maintain body temperature with a sheep skin placed over it like a sheet in order to reduce skin contact sensation is used. The enclosure is built to completely block out all light exposure and a random noise generator is used to drown out any distinguishable auditory stimulation.

The clients chosen to enter the SDC are the ones that are considered senior clients and have completed up to their eighth step in the Big Book. The procedure is designed to allow the patient to simply rest and open their thoughts to wherever their minds flow and has proven to be most helpful in finding answers or providing experiences that are pivotal in resolving those deep seeded issues that still haunt the addict. Unexpectedly, there has been a plethora of patients that use the SDC and only one has fallen asleep. Over 95 percent of the patients report very significant spiritual insight and valuable information gained for their life goals. Only two patients could not deal with the lack of stimulation in sensory deprivation and voluntarily exited the device after fifteen minutes. Since the participation is totally voluntary exiting the sensory deprivation chamber can be easily accomplished by pushing the door open; no disturbing incidence has ever occurred.

Note: Sensory deprivation has been used as a torture but those were involuntary programs for punishment and no exit was possible.

Neurotherapy

Neurotherapy is basically the same process as biofeedback except the subject is taught to train the brain in order to enhance brain frequencies by monitoring their EEG outputs. As Melinda Maxfield (ITP dissertation abstracts, 1990) demonstrated, once the patient is maximizing the theta range (4–8 cycles per second), there is an automatic shift into spiritual imagery. Many experiments have shown that neurotherapy creates the highest intuition and communication skills with others in this range of production (Braud and Anderson 1998).

Gonging Meditation

Most of the time humans are distracted from our present reality because of our perceived associations to the past or our fear association to the future. They have trained their brain so well that any event that happens in the present, whether imagined or real, creates so many associations that they lose the present and live in the past or future. For example, consider the person who receives a compliment for her shoes and is reminded of her first boyfriend or uncle who used to compliment her and manipulated her for abusive acts with his charm. Her first reaction is to fear the compliment and negate any positive emotion attached to the person or to herself. She therefore lives in the past. Another example is the person who hears the same compliment and imagines a major career boost for his charm and selection of clothes. Ego takes charge and he begins to demand others respect this aspect of him and cower to his authority. He lives in the future.

Mindful meditation is not relaxation or releasing the mind to wander whereever it wants to go, rather it is a focused concentration on some audible signal like a gong or the breath. Meditation teaches how to live in the moment and relish the experience of the time. People miss the wonderment of their lives and the costs of not being in the present can be high. People miss the sensations of their emotions and their smells and visions. Humans miss the breath of life and all the wonderful blessings they share. They miss the only time in which we they truly alive which is the present moment.

The goal is to train our minds to focus on the present and use the huge potential to access the inner forces that are on the edge of consciousness. The process is to focus on the present and now experience. This is a discipline with many rewards but has to be practiced. There is a monastery in India that requires its new monks to live in a cave for two years and just focus on their breath. This is meditation on the present and can be an excellent practice. The gonging meditation serves a similar objective. The person is charged to focus their attention on the gong and always come back to the gonging sound each and every time their thoughts drift away into the stories of their mind. It is difficult to master this discipline, yet the reports have been extremely favorable with descriptions of feeling rested and peaceful, hearing the words of God/Jesus/ Buddha/an angel. Meditations can be provided in which focusing on the present can be more immediately practiced on a daily basis. For example, focusing on how your feet feel as you walk across different surfaces can be quite amazing. Mindfulness is not just a practice in meditation but can become a way of living. Gong meditation can act as a tool to acquire this wonderful skill. For mindful meditation practices please refer to appendix A.

Vision Quest

In the story of Mona there is the description of a vision quest. Originally used by several cultures, it was intended to help the young citizen discover the mission he or she should play spiritually within the community. The brain is given priorities, and like learning to walk, the focus of a mission helps neuron patterns to form around the actions with many intermediate circuits as to how (motor circuits) and why (cognitive circuits) and when (planning circuits).

Finding a Safe Place

As the title provides, the goal of this imagery exercise is to find a magic safe place where the person can find peace. It can be a memory of a tree or a pond where the memories and related imagery can take you into peaceful tranquility. Memories are positive because the parameters are known and hopefully the scene is from before drug use when a person can still remember themselves as whole and love is a verb.

The other option is to build the "safe place" from fantasy, which is harder but more isolated from bad memories and distractions. There are more options to finding the right smells, the right feeling, the right vegetation and animals, flowers, and so on.

Entry into this safe place usually requires some guided instructions and accompanying rhythms, such as drumming or relaxing music, such as a flute and stringed instruments. Whenever stress is threatening, the person travels into their own personal safe place in their mind in order to relax and find peace and can serve as a boundary to fear.

Breathing Patterns

From the beginning of recorded history, breathing patterns have been used to enter a state of altered consciousness for spiritual practices. There are several methods but the one that has brought the most consistent success is merely stretching of the breathing cycles for longer counts. A further step would be to match the breathing cycle such that the same number of heart beats match each breathing cycle. The procedure is to begin the focus only on the breath without criticism of self or others, similar to the gonging focus in meditation. The correlation with the heart beat will hasten the unification of the body toward a shift in consciousness and spirituality. Prayer has been associated with this preparation, which helps not only in the reception of wisdom but also with the articulation of requests.

Drumming

Drumming a frequency of theta hertz (4–8 beats per second) will entrain the patient's brain toward spiritual thought patterns (Lawlis 1996) and has been used by most primitive cultures in the world. This stimulation is often maintained for twenty minutes in order for the patient to embrace the instructions of going into a spiritual journey and receiving valuable information. There is an overlap between using drums to entrain the brain to the lower frequencies and using training to obtain the same result.

It can be said that the drum is the horse that brings the person into the spiritual circle and if the feeling of being lost enters into one's fear, that one is reminded to find the horse (the beating of the drum) and the path will become clear. Drumming is merely the act of listening to the drums and allowing them to take one into spiritual space. That alone can be beneficial.

OVERALL THOUGHTS

It does not surprise the observer that the spiritual realm is so clearly the principal component in lifting the barriers as well as integrating into the Twelve Steps; however, as a neuro-scientist it has a profound underlying principle of being ever present in our brain structure as the source for our life direction. As if the ultimate treasure within our minds, it is supposedly an innate or even immortal part of us. However, like the primitive elements of our humanity there has to be an effort made, sometimes huge efforts, to discover our own healing force. Some humans have to struggle with fear, ego needs, ambivalence, damaged memories that haunt them, and physical illnesses that stand in their way to reach this source.

There are many thoughts and discussions held on this subject of finding the peace of the soul and enlightenment. Regardless of the struggle or the path, it seems easy to conclude that this is the destiny and mission that unites us all and our responsibility to help our brothers and sisters along the way, regardless of where people stand. That is the message for healing: that humans share our love from our deepest source of ourselves and make this the kind of world that is perceived as the heaven or after life that humans strive toward.

Afterword

A few years ago a new style that became very popular in the professional sector called *bioenergetics* emerged. Actually it was a form of psychoanalytic and body therapies introduced by Alexander Lowen which was initially conceived from the research of Wilhelm Reich (Lowen, A. 1994). It was a fascinating extension of Freud's thoughts about libido energy as a flow of vigor needed for the balance of life and that diseases like cancer could be healed if these energy flows were unblocked. Reich did some major research with this theory and Lowen developed it into a model for mental health.

These workshops were amazing with the techniques that released energies, but as with many models based on techniques, the less experienced and internal wisdom a person had, the more he or she relied on the techniques instead of the underlying intuition in the patient. The popularity became confused with the procedure and the excitement has dissipated largely because of the over focus on the techniques. The field is still alive and well, but the point of this chapter is that these techniques in brain plasticity should never be confused or become replacements for the central ingredients of human compassion and regard for the individual's path.

Success in therapeutic models, whether it is pharmacy, psychotherapy, hypnosis, behavior modification, or any known efforts in helping individuals is 90 percent based on the therapist's qualities of compassion and healing love. The ingredients of these interactive forces are empathy, unconditional regard, and genuineness. Psychoneuroplasticity is to be included in this category as a guiding principle toward change and transformation.

EMPATHY, UNCONDITIONAL REGARD, AND GENUINENESS

When a person enters the space for help, the first ten minutes of rapport are based on how much they feel understood, which leads to hope and safety. Degrees, certifications, prior endorsements, or any other signs of competence are distant seconds for that initial leap of faith into a contractual connection of trust. Empathy is that ability to communicate to a person in need that their emotional feelings and needs can be understood.

147

It should be clear that this does not mean that the therapist has to fully comprehend all situations or the conditions of the emotional turmoil, but to *communicate* the understanding of emotional feelings. It might be true that much of the therapy is an exploration of all levels of feelings and confusions, but it is the empathy toward clarification that deepens the safety and eventual positive transformational result.

In psychoneuroplasticity sessions, it becomes clear that as fears and releases into joy emerge, other barriers show themselves. Life problems are seldom one-dimensional. However, as the problems appear to be managed, competence and confidence grows.

Conditional regard is based on extending warmth and love based on a condition that must be met, such as promising to never embarrass, never getting pregnant or getting someone pregnant, always having a job, being obedient, and so on. Sometimes this last condition can enter the therapeutic situation by the unaware therapist: "I will help you on one condition that you get well and give me the credit." This leads to what may be called "transference" and often brings the destructive memories of no regard and caring from their childhood.

Unconditional regard is a bit more complex because of the coaching in the world to behave in specific ways for goals and the imperfect teachers humans are. The most grievous of parenting is to disregard their children's sense of self with early life messages, such as "You will never amount to anything" and equally destructive statements. The average person will quickly transfer the negative self-concept message to their own memory and negate themselves.

Like empathy, unconditional regard is the communication of care and love without conditions. However, as stated above, people are all conditioned to the concepts that they are rewarded for acting right and punished for wrong doing, so the acceptance of warmth and regard without having to earn it is very difficult to believe and accept. For example, to act disrespectfully and steal money or personal objects from the office and yet receive love and support for these acts, or in spite of them, can be very confusing if not destructive. This would be very important with enabling the addiction and allowing the disease to win.

But there is a distinction in accepting a person with full regard without having to accept their bad choices. There has to be consequences to bad choices, but that does not need to discredit a person's integrity. That seems to be a basic lesson in spiritual teaching, that it is the judgmental attitude and ego-based condemnation that is so damaging to a patient. The consistent attitude of the counselors have been examples of the long-term regard for the patients and the deep awareness of the struggles each person is going through that defines their poor judgments, not the elements of demonic genes.

Genuineness is the honesty of a relationship, but this does not mean opinions. Many people confuse what they think about other people as honest truths, such as "I think you are an idiot" or "People who believe that God exists are idiots." These are opinions and regardless of how much research is brought up, it is still an opinion. The only truth a person can share is data about him or herself because that person is the authority on oneself.

This rule goes for both sides of the desk, which includes the counselor or well-meaning helper. Opinions can be spoken but owned as opinions, genuineness is owned by the person speaking it, such as "This is my opinion that the more you express feeling depressed and down, the more you say bad things about me, but I know those are your opinions and I don't have to accept them as true."

As anyone in the business knows, the path to true transformation is honesty and openness to one's needs and choices. Lies exist in darkness and with light comes clarity. That light is the reassurance of hope and that secret lies, even by yourself, can be exposed into love and acceptance.

SUMMARY

The process of transformation has been discussed since the beginning of written history and with all the ideas floating around there are a few things common to all healing. There is love, either love from another or love from within. Either magnifies the other and it is presented through many guises, including sacrifice, the word, the touch, sacred rhythms, the spirit, and relationships. It can be modeled and attempts of articulating can be made. It can be seen in a million faces and examples, yet it is mysterious. Sometimes it is through the use of techniques that a healer can reveal the inner wisdom that holds the personal path of each of us at different times.

The truth has been made clear enough that there exists within each of us a glimpse of what the wondrous existence that can be our heaven but there are distractions of fear and distrust that hinder our paths. Addictive substances can also provide the denials of our true happiness by destructive crutches, and criminal thinking (obsessive thinking of possessions) can damage us to the far reaches of spirituality. There has yet to be seen someone who can't see the hope through the mist of fear and the injured soul, and that they can be worthy of love, peace, and following their true destiny.

Appendix A

General PNP Strategies

THE MINDFUL MEDITATION SERIES FOR RECOVERY

The recovery from any major life challenge, whether it be addiction, disease, trauma, grief, PTSD, chronic pain, or other categories of life struggle, there is a requirement for brain function transformation. This is because distinctive brain patterns form from either long term or injured methods of compensating for mental or physical pain. These patterns have to change in order to come into the natural rhythms of healing. The methods for change can come through spiritual conversion, direct disruption, and/or conscious re-training.

Mindful meditation has been used for centuries for transformation through the consciousness in restructuring the negative and distracting patterns. The basic principle of this form of meditation is to focus 100 percent of the time on the present, eliminating the past or future concerns. Too often memories of the past and worries about the future dominate our lives, creating needless stress and wasteful energy. We tend to repeat our obsessions of spiraling self-conflicts and erosions of discovery. The tremendous benefit of focusing on the present moment is the discovery and appreciation of the wonderful world in which we live and the participants in it. This is the space where choices are meaningful and critical to our quality of life.

The "Mindful Meditation Series for Recovery" exercises are not intended for the intensive process of learning meditation skills but are for the application of mindfulness to present circumstances. These have no prepared protocols other than to be practiced for a minimum of a day and maximum of seven days per exercise. They are designed from external to internal focus points but can be used in any order or selected by intention as conceived.

The intent of each exercise is evident by its content and the instructions can be articulated as needed for the person involved. The ultimate purposes are to appreciate the blessings we enjoy every moment of our lives and to realize the love of a higher life force.

THE GONGING MEDITATION CD

The Gonging Meditation CD is basically a cd with the sound of a ringing gong. It is used as a training project in which the subject is reminded throughout the process to focus on the sound of the gong. People usually emerge from the exercise feeling more relaxed and focused instead of feeling chaos and confusion.

RECOVERY MINDFUL TRAINING

Practice each of these exercises every week to increase your mindfulness in the external world:

Week 1: Focus on your Navel Center and Breathe—Become aware of your center, your navel. Whenever your mind wanders, bring your attention to your breath and center of gravity. Imagine that you have a balloon in your navel and each time you breathe in, the balloon inflates and each time you breathe out, the balloon deflates. Notice the colors of the balloon as you inhale and exhale.

Week 2: Undisclosed Acts of Kindness—Every day of this week engage in a secret act of kindness. It is important that you are anonymous so the act is not ego driven for recognition. These acts can be as simple or as complex as you would like.

Week 3: Walking Mindfully Side by Side—Walk next to another person side by side. Attempt to come to a pace that is comfortable for both without verbal communication. Notice how you feel while compromising your pace with the other person.

Week 4: Sympathetic Touch—Use a compassionate and loving touch with all things you handle or touch. Act as if you are handling a baby or an animal even with nonliving objects.

Week 5: Leave the World Better Than You Found It—Look for behaviors or ways to leave things or places better than you found them. Perhaps cleaner or happier than things were when you first visited. You can even use your smile to allow the energy of a room to be better than it was when you found it.

Week 6: Conscious Observation of Temperature—Move your consciousness to the temperature of your environment. When moving from room to room, inside to outside notice the change in the temperature your skin feels.

Week 7: Open Your Ears to Sounds—Several times a day stop and pay attention to sounds. Listen to obvious sounds around you and even in your body. Listen as if you are a stranger and are discovering these sounds for the first time. Pretend you are recording these sounds in your mind.

Week 8: Notice Vegetation—Become aware of all the greenery in your environment. Pay attention to the texture of leaves, color of bark, and size of plants. Gain an appreciation for the vegetation around you that supplies your body with oxygen. Begin to wonder what the vegetation would say around you if it could talk.

Week 9: Sky Gaze—Several times per day make it a point to gaze up into the sky or a room. See what new things you would notice in your surroundings. Notice the different shades of color the sky can become and what type of clouds are in the sky. At night, notice the moon and the stars. Appreciate that this is the first time the sky holds this exact shade at this exact moment.

Week 10: Evolution into New Places—As you walk through a door or opening into a new space, even from inside to outside, notice this transition and notice any sensations you may feel on the other side. Notice the temperature difference of the new room, the noise difference, the difference of smell, and the energy difference.

Week 11: Slow Down Your Stride—Walk at half the pace that you ordinarily would. Notice what happens to your state of mind when you slow down your pace. You may notice that your brain will follow your lead.

Week 12: Mindful Eating—Make sure that you are mindful with every bite you take. Enjoy what tastes and textures you are taking into your body. Open up all your senses as you eat or drink. Look at the colors, textures, and shapes of your food. Listen to the sounds of eating or drinking. Bite your food slower than you normally would.

Week 13: Love and Accept Your Body—Become aware this week of the movement of air in your body. For one week, practice love and kindness toward the body. Notice the feats that your body has done for you. Spend ten minutes each day reflecting on the gratitude your feel for your body. Inhale fresh air and as you exhale repeat the mantra "I appreciate my body."

Week 14: Exercise Your Facial Muscles—For one week, allow yourself to notice the different faces you make. Smile more than usual and notice every detail of your smile. Notice the emotions that arise each time your facial expression changes. Notice both the negative and positive of your facial expressions.

Week 15: Yes to Life—Proclaim "Yes" to everyone and everything that comes into your life. When you have the urge to disagree, reflect on whether the negation is really necessary and say yes instead.

Week 16: Stress Signals—Become aware of how you feel stress and what stress signals arise in your body. Notice all the body sensations, emotions, and thoughts that come up when stress arises. Pinpoint what stress signals your body gives at different levels of stress. Notice what makes you tense. Several times a day assess whether there is any anxiety in your body. Notice what relieves your stress and add these as your coping skills.

Week 17: Gratitude—Be curious and ask yourself at the beginning of the day and at night time "What am I grateful for?" This can be anything from an object, to a person, or a quality of yourself that you are thankful for. Write these things in a journal and continue to add to your list each day of the week.

The benefits of mindfulness training are vast from the simple concept of staying in tune with your conscious surroundings to a deep level of introspection and understanding of one's self. There is a mindful meditation class that is taught on a weekly basis that always opens up the perception of how powerful mindful meditation actually is. The groups of clients come together every Monday with their mindful meditation assignment in hand, full of journal entries of their personal experience from the week before, hungry for a new mindful task. The clients start by sharing their experience from the week before. On one occasion, we were discussing the exercise "Star Gaze" and it was Meredith's turn to share. Meredith was a shy and unsure fifty-six-year-old woman who had shared before that she never felt important to anyone and practically did not know what value felt like within herself. Meredith's face became serious as she shared a beautiful piece of poetry she came up with from the mindfulness of looking up into the sky. Meredith's face filled with tears and said this inspiration was great for her, she realized by looking up and opening up her perspective that she was actually connected to the universe, making her a piece of the beauty around her. Meredith was finally able to be coherent to her amazing value in the universe. These introspective realizations are often told. After the clients all share their experience from the week before, they read their new assignment in silence and then share what their impression of the exercise is. On this particular Monday the new assignment was "Leave the World Better Than You Found It." Julie shared her perspective of the assignment. She explained that before she came to our facility she was always leaving the world worse than she found it because she sold drugs without any consciousness of what effect this would have. Julie opened up and said she feels a sense of guilt because of this and finds this mindfulness assignment to be an exact opposite of what she used to live by. She felt this assignment would be powerful for her because it would be a mindful reminder of the fact that she can make this world a better place and she was not doomed by her past. We designed our groups to be a sacred safe place to do individual mindfulness work and then come back to center with a group of compassionate people that one could process with. The clients pour their hearts and souls into the mindfulness training and found it paid off. Leah said in particular "I learned that my emotions are okay to feel, that I could hold space for any stimulus that would come my way, and most importantly that my higher power would not give me anything I could not handle. I did not have to disassociate to protect myself anymore." The clients found the value of staying grounded and present in the world around them because essentially that was the only time they were actually living.

Appendix B

Modified Ketogenic Foods

SAFE FOODS

Beef, Steak, Hamburger, Prime Rib, Filet Mignon, Roast Beef, Chicken, Duck, Any Fish, Tuna, Salmon, Trout, Halibut, Lamb, Pork, Bacon, Ham, Eggs, Shrimp, Crab, Lobster, Butter, Oils (Olive Oil, Flaxseed Oil, etc.), Mustard, Salt, Pepper, Soy Sauce, Tea, Coffee, Heavy Cream, and Saccharin

MINIMAL CARB FOODS (LIMITED QUANTITIES ONLY)

Broccoli, Spinach, Lettuce, Cabbage, Bok Choy, Kale, Asparagus, Mustard Greens, Mushrooms, Cucumbers, Pickles, Celery, Green Beans, Brussel Sprouts, Cauliflower, Artichokes, Peppers (Red, Green, Jalapeno, Habanero), Onions, Sprouts (Bean, Alfalfa, etc.), Radicchio and Endive, Herbs (Parsley, Cilantro, Basil, Rosemary, and Thyme), Radishes, Sea Vegetables, Jicama, Avocado, Asparagus, Green Beans and Wax Beans, Broccoli, Summer Squash, Zuchinni, Scallions or Green Onions, Bamboo Shoots, Leeks, Brussels Sprouts, Snow Peas (pods), Tomatoes, Eggplant, Tomatillos, Artichokes, Fennel, Okra*, Spaghetti Squash, Celery Root (Celeriac), Turnip, Water Chestnuts, Pumpkin*, Nuts, Flaxseeds, Cheeses, Salami, Pastrami, Hot Dogs, Sausages, Ribs (watch out for the sauce!), Buffalo Wings, Liverwurst, Oysters, Abalone, Protein Powders, Sugar-Free Jello, and Salad Dressings (some)

HIGHER CARB FOODS (VERY LIMITED QUANTITIES)

Grapefruit, Lemons, Limes, Strawberries, Olives, Rasberries, Blackberries, Kiwis*, Plums, Oranges, Pears, Pineapple, and Corn

FOODS THAT ARE NOT APPROPRIATE

Bread, Cereal, Rice, Potatoes, Corn Peas, Candy, Cake, Cheesecake, Biscuits, Donuts, Fruit Juices, High Carb Fruits, Pastries, Soft Drinks, Rolls, Bagels, Popcorn, Battered Foods (Fried Chicken, etc.), Gravy, Sugar, Milk Chocolate, and Corn Syrup

Appendix C

PNP Approaches to Barriers to Sobriety Check List

ANXIETY BARRIER

Signs and Symptoms :

- Concentration challenges ( )
- Worries excessively ( )
- States of panic of loss of control ( )
- Headaches and high blood pressure ( )
- Restlessness ( )
- Easily fatigued ( )
- Difficulty sleeping and disturbed sleep pattern ( )
- Muscle tension ( )
- Afflicted by negative messages that are held in cognition ( )

Protocols for Anxiety:

- BAUD desensitization to negative cognitions ( )
- BAUD for relaxation ( )
- Music stimulation ( )
- Breathing techniques ( )
- Biofeedback ( )
- Meditation practice ( )
- Laughter ( )
- Nutritional diet ( )
- CD#1 "Breathing Meditation" ( )

PTSD BARRIER

Signs and Symptoms:

- Anxiety ( )
- Trauma kept in memory and experienced by cues and nightmares ( )
- Heightened emotional complexity when memory is re-lived ( )

Protocols for PTSD:

- BAUD for memory desensitization ( )
- Safe place imagery ( )
- Biofeedback ( )
- Hyperbaric chamber ( )

DEPRESSION BARRIER

Signs and Symptoms:

- Poor or shallow sleep cycles ( )
- Unstable emotional states ( )
- Concentration challenges ( )
- Loss of joy ( )
- Feeling of despair and hopelessness ( )
- Numbness of emotions ( )
- No existential reason or mission in life ( )

Protocols:

- BAUD to increase joy in pleasure centers ( )
- CD #2 "Unity and Joy" ( )
- Exercise ( )
- Laughter ( )
- Learning a new skill or ability ( )
- Fulfilling a "bucket" in life ( )
- Posturing ( )
- Blue lights and chewing gum ( )
- Nutritional diet and supplements ( )
- Twenty qualities exercise ( )

DEPRESSION WITH INTRUDING MESSAGES BARRIER

Signs and Symptoms:

- Rumination or obsessive memories of criticism or judgment ( )
- Self-induced guilt ( )
- Low self-esteem ( )
- Low frustration tolerance ( )
- Anxiety regarding performance ( )
- Depression regarding no perceived reinforcement ( )
- Possibly immune to psychological reasoning ( )

Protocols:

- BAUD for neutralizing high emotional triggers to memories ( )
- Redirecting emotional response with powerful aromas ( )
- CD#2 "Unity and Joy" ( )

- Rhythmic exercise ( )
- Mental rehearsal ( )
- Breathing techniques ( )
- Chanting in repetition ( )
- Neurotherapy ( )
- Symbolic imagery for twenty-one days ( )
- Mindful meditation ( )
- Nutritional diet ( )

MULTI-POLAR/RAGE BARRIER

Signs and Symptoms :

- Range of moods from rage to deep depression ( )
- Muscle tension ( )
- Large variation in blood pressure ( )
- Intense anxiety to triggers ( )
- Environmental and people scanning for stress
- Brain inflammation ( )
- Rage triggers ( )
- Low frustration tolerance ( )

Protocols for Multi-Polar/ Rage Barrier:

- BAUD for relaxation ( )
- Neurotherapy ( )
- Hyperbaric chamber ( )
- Rhythmic exercise such as tai chi and yoga ( )
- Entrainment by listening to relaxation CDs ( )
- Mental rehearsal ( )
- Chewing gum ( )
- Biofeedback ( )
- Breathing techniques ( )
- Chanting and mantras ( )
- CDs for proper sleep cycle ( )
- Positive reinforcement ( )

SPIRITUAL BLOCKAGE BARRIER

Signs and Symptoms:

- Blocked to finding inner wisdom ( )
- Self-serving needs are focused on/ego driven ( )
- Sense of being lost in life with no values to defend ( )
- Restlessness ( )
- Anxious about value of life ( )

- Depressed over no mission or passion ( )
- Feeling of disconnection from others or spiritual concepts ( )
- Delusional thinking as to sense of self ( )
- Control driven to false security ( )

Protocol to Spiritual Blockage:

- Find a safe place with imagery ( )
- Sensory deprivation chamber ( )
- Neurotherapy ( )
- Gong meditation ( )
- Vision quest ( )
- Breathing techniques ( )
- Listening to drumming ( )

References

ADAA. (2007). Stress and anxiety disorders study. Silver Spring, MD: *Anxiety Disorders of America.*

Adler, A. (2011). *The Practice and Theory of Individual Psychology.* Mansfield Centre, CT: Martino.

Aftanas, L., and Golosheykin, S. (2005). Impact of regular meditation practice on EEG activity at rest and during evoked negative emotions. *International Journal of Neuroscience* 115(6), 893–909.

Alcoholics Anonymous. (1976). *Alcoholics Anonymous.* New York: Alcoholics Anonymous.

Allman, J. M., Hakeem, A., Erwin, J. M., Nimchinsky, E., and Hof, P. (2001). The anterior. *Annals of the New York Academy of Science* 935, 107–117.

Alschuler, K. N., Theisen-Goodvich, M. E., Haig, A. J., and Geisser, M. E. (2008). A comparison of the relationship between depression, perceived disability, and physical performance in persons with chronic pain. *European Journal of Pain* Aug 12(6): 757–764.

American College of Rheumatology (2000, November 1). Abnormal pain memory helps to explain fibromyalgia. *ScienceDaily.*

American Psychiatric Association. (2000). *Diagnostic and Statistical Manual of Mental Disorders.* Arlington, VA: American Psychiatric Association.

ASAM (American Society of Addiction Medicine). (1996). Patient placement criteria for the treatment of substance-related disorders. Chevy Chase, MD: *American Society of Addiction Medicine.*

Andrews, T. (2010). *Animal Speak.* St.Paul, MN: Llewellyn Worldwide.

Avitsur, R., Hunzeker, J., and Sheridan, J. F. Role of early stress in the individual differences in host response to viral infection. Philadelphia, PA: *Brain, Behavior, and Immunity* 20, no. 4 (2006): 339–348.

Barak, S., Liu, F., Hamida, S. B., Yowell, Q. V., Neasta, J., Kharazia, V., . . . and Ron, D. (2013). Disruption of alcohol-related memories by mTORC1 inhibition prevents relapse. *Nature Neuroscience* 16(8), 1111–1117.

Bays, J. C., M. D. (2011). *How to Train a Wild Elephant: And Other Adventures in Mindfulness.* Boston, MA: Shambhala Publications.

Begley, S. (2004). Scans of monks' brains show meditation alters structure, functioning. *Wall Street Journal* 5.

Bible, H. (1984). New international version. Grand Rapids, MI: *Zondervan.*

Biederman, J., Wilens, T., Mick, E., Milberger, S., Spencer, T. J., and Faraone, S. V. (1995). Psychoactive substance use disorders in adults with attention deficit hyperactivity disorder (ADHD): effects of ADHD and psychiatric comorbidity. Arlington, VA: *American Journal of Psychiatry* 152, no. 11: 1652–1658.

Bittman, B., Berk, L., Shannon, M., Sharaf, M., Westengard, J., Guegler, K. J., et al. (2005). Recreational music-making modulates the human stress response: A preliminary individualized gene expression strategy. Smithtown, NY: *Medical Science Monitor* 11(2), BR31–40.

Blair, A., Hall, C., and Leyshon, G. (1993). Imagery effects on the performance of skilled and novice soccer players. *Journal of Sports Sciences* 11(2), 95–101.

Blum, K., Chen, A. L. C., Braverman, E. R., Comings, D. E., Chen, T. J., Arcuri, V., and Oscar-Berman, M. (2008). Attention-deficit-hyperactivity disorder and reward deficiency syndrome. United Kingdom: *Neuropsychiatric Disease and Treatment* Oct 4(5): 893–918.

Braud, W., and Anderson, R. (Eds.). (1998). *Transpersonal Research Methods for the Social Sciences: Honoring Human Experience*. New York: Sage Publications.

Breach, N. B. (2012). Heart rate variability biofeedback in the treatment of major depression (Doctoral dissertation, Rutgers, The State University of New Jersey).

Brené, S., Bjørnebekk, A., Åberg, E., Mathé, A. A., Olson, L., and Werme, M. (2007). Running is rewarding and antidepressive. Philadelphia, PA: *Physiology and Behavior* 92(1), 136–140.

Brunet, A., Orr, S.P., Tremblay, J., Robertson, K., Nader, K., and Pitman, R. K. (2008). Effect of Post-retrieval propranolol on psychophysiological responding during subsequent script-driven traumatic imagery in post-traumatic stress disorder. Philadelphia PA : *Journal of Psychiatric Research* May, 42(6): 503–506.

Bruursema, R. (2013). Bio-acoustical neuromodulation for phobia and excessive anxiety reduction. *University of Kansas Medical Center*.

Bryant, R. A., Sutherland, K., and Guthrie, R. M. (2007). Impaired specific autobiographical memory as a risk factor for posttraumatic stress after trauma. *Journal of Abnormal Psychology* Vol. 116(4), 837–841.

Buzsaki, G. (2006) *Rhythms of the Brain*. Oxford: Oxford University Press.

Cabrera, M. A. S., Mesas, A. E., Garcia, A. R. L., and de Andrade, S. M. (2007). Malnutrition and depression among community-dwelling elderly people. *Journal of the American Medical Directors Association, 8*(9), 582–584.

Cahn, B. R., and Polich, J. (2006). Meditation states and traits: EEG, ERP, and neuroimaging studies. Washington, D.C.: *Psychological Bulletin* 132(2), 180.

Calmels, C., Berthoumieux, C., and d'Arripe-Longueville, F. (2004). Effects of an imagery training program on selective attention of national softball players. *Sport Psychologist* 18(3).

Carmeli, E. (2014). Aging, neuroplasticity and neuro rehabilitation. Foster City, CA : *Journal of Aging Science*.

Carmody, J., and Baer, R. A. (2008). Relationships between mindfulness practice and levels of mindfulness, medical and psychological symptoms and well-being in a mindfulness-based stress reduction program. *Journal of Behavioral Medicine* 31.1: 23–33.

Cartwright, D. (2002). The narcissistic exoskeleton: The defensive organization of the rage-type murderer. Houston, TX: *Bulletin of the Menninger Clinic* 66(1), 1–18.

Chaouloff, F. (1989). Physical exercise and brain monoamines: A review. *Acta Physiologica Scandinavica* 137(1), 1–13.

Chapell, M. S. (1994). Inner speech and respiration: Toward a possible mechanism of stress reduction. Missoula, MT: *Percept Mot Skills* 79(2), 803–811.

Christie, W., and Moore, C. (2005). The impact of humor on patients with cancer. Pittsburgh, PA: *Clin J Oncol Nurs, 9*(2), 211–218.

Cohen, S., Levi-Montalcini, R., and Hamburger, V. (1954). A nerve growth-stimulating factor isolated from sarcom as 37 and 180. Washington, D.C.: *Proceedings of the National Academy of Sciences of the United States of America* 40(10), 1014.

Costello, R. M., Lawlis, G. F., Manders, K. R., and Celistino, J. F. (1978). Empirical derivation of a partial personality typology of alcoholics. *Journal of Studies on Alcohol and Drugs* 39(07), 1258.

Cotman, C. W., and Berchtold, N. C. (2002). Exercise: A behavioral intervention to enhance brain health and plasticity. *Trends in Neurosciences* 25(6), 295–301.

Cotman, C. W., Berchtold, N. C., and Christie, L. A. (2007). Exercise builds brain health: Key roles of growth factor cascades and inflammation. *Trends in Neurosciences* 30(9), 464–472.

Critchley, H. D., Melmed, R. N., Featherstone, E., Mathias, C. J., and Dolan, R. J. (2001). Brain activity during biofeedback relaxation: A functional neuroimaging investigation. *Brain* 124(5), 1003–1012.

Csef, H., and Hefner, J. (2006). [Psychosocial stress as a risk- and prognostic factor in coronary artery disease and myocardial infarction]. *Versicherungsmedizin, 58*(1), 3–8.

Dahl, R. E. (2004). Adolescent brain development: a period of vulnerabilities and opportunities. Keynote address. New York: *Annals of the New York Academy of Sciences* 1021.1: 1–22.

Davidson, R. J., Kabat-Zinn, J., Schumacher, J., Rosenkranz, M., Muller, D., Santorelli, S. F., and Sheridan, J. F. (2003). Alterations in brain and immune function produced by mindfulness meditation. Tampa, FL: *Psychosomatic Medicine* 65(4), 564–570.

Davidson, R. J., and Lutz, A. (2008). Buddha's brain: Neuroplasticity and meditation. *IEEE Signal Processing Magazine, 25*(1), 176.

Debiee, J., Doyere, V., Nader, K., and Ledoux, J. E. (2006). Directly reactivated, but not indirectly reactivated, memories undergo reconsolidation in the amygdala Washington, D.C.: *Proceedings of the National Academy of Sciences of the U.S.A.* Feb. 28; 103 (9):3428–3433.

Dickens, C. (2009). *A Christmas Carol.* New York: Random House.

Dictionary.com, LLC. Spirituality Definition.

Doidge, N. (2007) *The Brain That Changes Itself.* New York: Penguin.

Dörfel, Denise; Werner, et al. (2010). Pilot neuroimaging study in civilian trauma survivors: Episodic recognition memory, hippocampal volume, and posttraumatic stress disorder symptom severity. Philadelphia, PA: *Zeitschrift für Psychologie/Journal of Psychology* Vol. 218(2), 128–134.

Dossey, L. (1997). *Be Careful What You Pray For.* San Francisco: Harper.

———. (1984). *Beyond Illness.* Boston: New Science Library.

———. (2006.) *The Extraordinary Healing Power of Ordinary Things.* New York: Harmony/Random House.

———. (2001). *Healing Beyond the Body: Medicine and the Infinite Reach of the Mind.* Boston: Shambhala Publications.

———. (1993) *Healing Words: The Power of Prayer in the Practice of Medicine.* San Francisco: Harper.

———. (2009) *The Power of Premonitions: How Knowing the Future Can Shape Our Lives.* New York: Dutton.

———. (1996). *Prayer Is Good Medicine.* San Francisco: Harper.

———. (1989). *Recovering the Soul.* New York: Bantam.

———. (1999). *Reinventing Medicine.* San Francisco: Harper.

Edwards, L. (2011). Biofeedback, meditation, and mindfulness. West Olive, MI: *Biofeedback* 39(2), 67–70.

Esch, T., Duckstein, J., Welke, J., and Braun, V. (2007). Mind/body techniques for physiological and psychological stress reduction: Stress management via Tai Chi training—a pilot study. Smithtown, NY: *Medical Science Monitor* 13(11), CR488–497.

Farb, N. A., Segal, Z. V., Mayberg, H., Bean, J., McKeon, D., Fatima, Z., and Anderson, A. K. (2007). Attending to the present: mindfulness meditation reveals distinct neural modes of self-reference. Cary, NC: *Social Cognitive and Affective Neuroscience* 2(4), 313–322.

Flora, S. J. (2007). Role of free radicals and antioxidants in health and disease. Poitiers Cédex, France: *Cell Mol Biol (Noisy-le-grand), 53*(1), 1–2.

Floresco, S. B., and Ghods-Sharifi, S. (2007). Amygdala-prefrontal cortical circuitry regulates effort-based decision making. Cary, NC: *Cerebral Cortex* 17 (2): 251–260. doi:10.1093/cercor/bhj143. PMID 16495432.

Flory, K., Molina, B. S., Pelham, W. E., Jr., Gnagy, E., and Smith, B. (2006). Childhood ADHD predicts risky sexual behavior in young adulthood. *Journal of Clinical Child and Adolescent Psychology* 35(4), 571–577.

Foote, B., Smolin, Y., Neft, D. I., and Lipschitz, D. (2008). Dissociative disorders and suicidality in psychiatric outpatients. Philadelphia, PA: *Journal of Nervous and Mental Disease* 196(1), 29–36.

Frankland, P. W., Bontempi, B., Talton, L. E., Kaczmarek, L., and Silva, A. J. (2004). The involvement of the anterior cingulate cortex in remote contextual fear memory. *Science, 304*(5672), 881–883.

Franks, S. (2011). Stomp For Life Program. University of North Texas. Denton, TX: *Primary Care Research Journal.*

Freeman, L. and Lawlis, F. *Mosby's Complementary and Alternative Medicine* (2001) St. Louis: Mosby.

Freud, S. (1920). *A General Introduction to Psychoanalysis.* New York: Boni and Liveright.

Garland, E. L., and Howard, M. O. (2009). Neuroplasticity, psychosocial genomics, and the biopsychosocial paradigm in the 21st century. Cary, NC: *Health and Social Work* 34(3), 191–199.

Gatchel, R. J., Hatch, J. P., Maynard, A., Turns, R., Taunton-Blackwood, A. (1979). Comparison of heart rate biofeedback, false biofeedback, and systematic desensitization in reducing speech anxiety: Short- and long-term effectiveness. Washington, D.C.: *Journal of Consulting and Clinical Psychology* Vol. 47(3), 1979; 620–627.

Glickman, G., Byrne, B., Pineda, C., Hauck, W. W., and Brainard, G. C. (2006). Light therapy for seasonal affective disorder with blue narrow-band light-emitting diodes (LEDs). Philadelphia, PA: *Biological Psychiatry* 59(6), 502–507.

Gómez-Pinilla, F. (2008). Brain foods: the effects of nutrients on brain function. London: *Nature Reviews Neuroscience* 9.7: 568–578.

Gordon, S. M., Tulak, F., and Troncale, J. (2004). Prevalence and characteristics of adolescents patients with co-occurring ADHD and substance dependence. *Journal of Addictive Diseases* 23(4), 31–40.

Haast, R. A., and Kiliaan, A. J. (2014). Impact of fatty acids on brain circulation, structure and function. Philadelphia PA: *Prostaglandins, Leukotrienes and Essential Fatty Acids (PLEFA).*

Hall, C., Schmidt, D., Durand, M., and Buckolz, E. (1994). Imagery and motor skills acquisition. Boston, MA: *Imagery in Sports and Physical Performance,* 121–134.

Hammond, D. C. (2003). QEEG-guided neurofeedback in the treatment of obsessive compulsive disorder. *Journal of Neurotherapy* 7(2), 25–52.

Harner, M. J., Mishlove, J., and Bloch, A. (1990). *The Way of the Shaman.* San Francisco, CA: Harper and Row.

Harris, C. A., and D'Eon, J. L. (2007). Psychometric properties of the Beck Depression Inventory-Second Edition (BDI-II) in individuals with chronic pain. Philadelphia, PA: *Pain.*

Hasenkamp, W., and Barsalou, L. W. (2012). Effects of meditation experience on functional connectivity of distributed brain networks. Switzerland: *Frontiers in Human Neuroscience* 6, 38.

Hawkes, C. H., and Doty, R. L. (2009). *The Neurology of Olfaction.* New York: Cambridge University Press.

HeartMath, LLC. (2014). Boulder Creek, CA: *HeartMath LLC.*

Hölzel, B. K., Carmody, J., Vangel, M., Congleton, C., Yerramsetti, S. M., Gard, T., and Lazar, S. W. (2011). Mindfulness practice leads to increases in regional brain gray matter density. Philadelphia, PA: *Psychiatry Research: Neuroimaging* 191(1), 36–43.

Hölzel, B. K., Ott, U., Hempel, H., Hackl, A., Wolf, K., Stark, R., and Vaitl, D. (2007). Differential engagement of anterior cingulate and adjacent medial frontal cortex in adept meditators and non-meditators. *Neuroscience Letters* 421(1): 16–21.

Hunzeker, J., Padgett, D. A., Sheridan, P. A., Dhabhar, F. S., and Sheridan, J. F. (2004). Modulation of natural killer cell activity by restraint stress during an influenza A/PR8 infection in mice. Philadelphia, PA: *Brain, Behavior, and Immunity* 18(6), 526–535.

Hwang, J. H. (2006). [The effects of the inhalation method using essential oils on blood pressure and stress responses of clients with essential hypertension]. Korea: Taehan Kanho Hakhoe Chi, 36(7), 1123–1134.

Johnstone, J., Gunkelman, J., Lunt, J. (2005). Links clinical database development: Characterization of EEG phenotypes. Burbank, CA: *Clinical EEG and Neuroscience,* Apr 36(2):99–107.

Jones, S., and Bonci, A. (2005). Synaptic plasticity and drug addiction. Philadelphia, PA: *Current Opinion in Pharmacology* 5 (1): 20–5. doi:10.1016/j.coph.2004.08.011. PMID 15661621.

Jung, C. G. (1976). *The Symbolic Life: Miscellaneous Writings* (p. 345). Princeton University Press.

———. (1957). *The Undiscovered Self.* New York: Signet.

Kalivas, P. W., and Volkow, N. D. (2005). The neural basis of addiction: a pathology of motivation and choice. Arlington, VA: *Journal of Psychiatry* 162 (8): 1403–13. doi:10.1176/appi.ajp.162.8.1403. PMID 16055761.

Kaltenbach, K., Berghella, V., and Finnegan, L. (1998). Opioid dependence during pregnancy: Effects and management. Philadelphia, PA: *Obstetrics and Gynecology Clinics of North America* 25(1), 139–151.

Karashima, A., Katayama, N., and Nakao, M. (2010). Enhancement of synchronization between hippocampal and amygdala theta waves associated with pontine wave density. Bethesda, MD: *Journal of Neurophysiology* May; 103(5): 2318–2325.

Keating, D. P., Lerner, R. M., and Steinberg, L. (2004). Cognitive and brain development. Hoboken, NJ : *Handbook of Adolescent Psychology* 2, 45–84.

Khantzian, E. J. (2003). Understanding addictive vulnerability: An evolving psychodynamic perspective. London: *Neuropsychoanalysis: An Interdisciplinary Journal for Psychoanalysis and the Neurosciences* 5(1), 5–21.

Kjellgren, A., Bood, S. A., Axelsson, K., Norlander, T., and Saatcioglu, F. (2007). Wellness through a comprehensive Yogic breathing program: A controlled pilot trial. London: *BMC Complementry and Alternative Medicine* 7(1), 43.

Klassen, A. F., Miller, A., and Fine, S. (2004). Health-related quality of life in children and adolescents who have a diagnosis of attention-deficit/hyperactivity disorder. Washington, D.C.: *Pediatrics, 114*(5), e541–547.

Kleen, M., and Reitsma, B. (2011). Appliance of heart rate variability biofeedback in Acceptance and Commitment Therapy: A pilot study. United Kingdom: *Journal of Neurotherapy* 15(2), 170–181.

Kleshchevnikov, A. M. (1999). Synaptic plasticity in the hippocampus during afferent activation reproducing the pattern of the theta rhythm. New York, NY: *Neuroscience and Behavioral Physiology* Mar–Apr; 29(2):185–96.

Klevens, R. M., Hu, D. J., Jiles, R., and Holmberg, S. D. (2012). Evolving epidemiology of hepatitis C virus in the United States. Cary, NC: *Clinical infectious diseases,* 55(suppl 1), S3–S9.

Kourrich, S., Rothwell, P. E., Klug, J. R., Thomas, M. J. (2007). Cocaine experience controls bidirectional synaptic plasticity in the nucleus accumbens. Washington, D.C.: *Journal of Neuroscience* 27 (30): 7921–8. doi:10.1523/JNEUROSCI.1859–07.2007. PMID 17652583.

Krauss, M. R., Russell, R. K., Powers, T. E., and Li, Y. (2006). Accession standards for attention-deficit/hyperactivity disorder: A survival analysis of military recruits, 1995–2000. Bethesda, MD: *Military Medicine, 171*(2), 99–102.

Kresina, T. F., Khalsa, J., Cesari, H., and Francis, H. (2005). Hepatitis C virus infection and substance abuse: Medical management and developing models of integrated care—an introduction. Cary, NC: *Clinical Infectious Diseases* 40(Supplement 5), S259–S262.

Krikorian, R., Shidler, M. D., Dangelo, K., Couch, S. C., Benoit, S. C., and Clegg, D. J. (2012). Dietary ketosis enhances memory in mild cognitive impairment. Philadelphia, PA: *Neurobiology of Aging* 33(2), 425–e19.

Labbe, E., Schmidt, N., Babin, J., and Pharr, M. (2007). Coping with stress: The effectiveness of different types of music. Wheat Ridge, CO: *Applied Psychophysiology Biofeedback* 32(3–4), 163–168.

Laporte, L., and Guttman, H. (2001). Abusive relationships in families of women with borderline personality disorder, anorexia nervosa and a control group. Philadelphia, PA: *Journal of Nervous and Mental Disease* 189(8), 522–531.

Lawlis, F. (2004). *The ADD Answer: How to Help Your Child Now.* New York, NY: Penguin.

———. (2010). An international study on effectiveness of sonic management (BAUD). *Proceedings of ISNR*, 2010, Denver, Colorado.

———. (2002). *Imagery Journey into Transformation.* Unpublished.

———. (2006). *The IQ Answer.* New York: Viking.

———. (2007). *Mending the Broken Bond: The 90-day Answer to Developing a Loving Relationship with Your Child.* New York, NY: Penguin.

———. (2009). *Retraining the Brain: A 45-day Plan to Conquer Stress and Anxiety.* New York: Penguin Group.

———. (2008). *The Stress Answer.* New York: Viking.

———. (1996). *Transpersonal Medicine.* Boston: Shambhala

Lawlis, G. F., and Rubin, S. E. (1971). 16-PF study of personality patterns in alcoholics. New Jersey: *Quarterly Journal of Studies on Alcohol* 32(2), 318–327.

Lazar, S. W., Bush, G., Gollub, R. L., Fricchione, G. L., Khalsa, G., and Benson, H. (2000). Functional brain mapping of the relaxation response and meditation. New York, NY: *Neuroreport*, 11(7), 1581–1585.

Lehrer, J. (2012). The Forgetting Pill: How a new drug can target specific memories—And erase them forever. *Wired-New York*, 84.

Lehrer, P. M., Vaschillo, E., Vaschillo, B., Lu, S. E., Eckberg, D. L., Edelberg, R., . . . and Hamer, R. M. (2003). Heart rate variability biofeedback increases baroreflex gain and peak expiratory flow. Tampa, FL: *Psychosomatic Medicine* 65(5), 796–805.

Lerner, R. M., Boyd, M. J., and Du, D. (1998). Adolescent development. New York: *Corsini Encyclopedia of Psychology.*

Levine, S. (2009). *A Year to Live: How to Live This Year as if It Were Your Last.* New York: Random House LLC.

Levitin, D. (2007) *This Is Your Brain on Music* New York: Penguin Group.

Li, J. Z., Bunney, B. G., Meng, F., Hagenauer, M. H., Walsh, D. M., Vawter, M. P., . . . and Bunney, W. E. (2013). Circadian patterns of gene expression in the human brain and disruption in major depressive disorder. *Proceedings of the National Academy of Sciences,* 110(24), 9950–9955.

Lilly, J. C. (1977). *The Deep Self: Profound Relaxation and the Tank Isolation Technique.* New York: Simon and Schuster.

Lippincott Williams and Wilkins. Addiction Definition. http://www.medilexicon.com/medicaldictionary.php?t=1061. (2006).

Locke J., Berkeley, G., and Hume, D. (1961). *The Empiricists.* New York: Anchor Books.

Loftis, J. M., and Huckans, M. (2013). Substance use disorders: Psychoneuroimmunological mechanisms and new targets for therapy. Philadelphia, PA: *Pharmacology and Therapeutics* 139(2), 289–300.

Lowen, A. (1994). *Bioenergetics: The Revolutionary Therapy That Uses the Language of the Body to Heal the Problems of the Mind.* New York, NY: Arkana.

Luders, E., Toga, A. W., Lepore, N., and Gaser, C. (2009). The underlying anatomical correlates of long-term meditation: Larger hippocampal and frontal volumes of gray matter. Philadelphia, PA: *Neuroimage* 45(3), 672–678.

Lutz, A., Greischar, L. L., Rawlings, N. B., Ricard, M., and Davidson, R. J. (2004). Long-term meditators self-induce high-amplitude gamma synchrony during mental practice. Washington, D.C.: *Proceedings of the National Academy of Sciences of the U.S.A.* 101(46), 16369–16373.

Manna, A., Raffone, A., Perrucci, M. G., Nardo, D., Ferretti, A., Tartaro, A., . . . and Romani, G. L. (2010). Neural correlates of focused attention and cognitive monitoring in meditation. Philadelphia, PA: *Brain Research Bulletin* 82(1), 46–56.

Maxfield, M. C. (1990). *Effects of Rhythmic Drumming on EEG and Subjective Experience* (Doctoral dissertation, Institute of Transpersonal Psychology).

McTaggart, L. (2007) *The Intention Experiment*. New York: Free Press.

Meeusen, R., and De Meirleir, K. (1995). Exercise and brain neurotransmission. *Sports Medicine* 20(3), 160–188.

Merzenich, M. M., Nelson, R. J., Stryker, M. P., Cynader, M. S., Schoppmann, A., and Zook, J. M. (1984). Somatosensory cortical map changes following digit amputation in adult monkeys. *Journal of Comparative Neurology* 224(4), 591–605.

Mifflin, H. (2000). *The American Heritage Dictionary of the English Language*. Boston, MA: Houghton Mifflin.

Miller, G. E., Cohen, S., Pressman, S., Barkin, A., Rabin, B. S., and Treanor, J. J. (2004). Psychological stress and antibody response to influenza vaccination: when is the critical period for stress, and how does it get inside the body? Tampa, FL: *Psychosomatic Medicine* 66(2), 215–223.

Miller, J. J., Fletcher, K., and Kabat-Zinn, J. (1995). Three-year follow-up and clinical implications of a mindfulness meditation-based stress reduction intervention in the treatment of anxiety disorders. Philadelphia, PA: *General Hospital Psychiatry* 17(3), 192–200.

Miller, N. E. (1978). Biofeedback and visceral learning. Palo Alto, CA : *Annual Review of Psychology* 29(1), 373–404.

Miller, W. R., and Rollnick, S. (2002). *Motivational Interviewing: Preparing People for Change*. New York: Guilford Press.

MindBodySeries.com | Health and Wellness Multi-Media Programs. (n.d.). MindBodySeriescom. Retrieved July 29, 2014, from http://www.mindbodyseries.com/.

Mischoulon, D., and Raab, M. F. (2007). The role of folate in depression and dementia. Memphis, TN: *Journal of Clinical Psychiatry* 68 Suppl 10, 28–33.

Murphy, M., and White, R. A. (1978). *The Psychic Side of Sports*. Reading, MA: Addison-Wesley.

Musselman, D. L., Evans, D. L., and Nemeroff, C. B. (1998). The relationship of depression to cardiovascular disease: epidemiology, biology, and treatment. Chicago, IL: *Archives of General Psychiatry* 55(7), 580–592.

Nader, K., Schafe, G., and LeDoux, J. E. Fear memories require protein synthesis in the amygdala for reconsolidation after retrieval. United Kingdom: *Nature*, Aug.17 2000, 406 (6797): 722–726.

National Institute on Drug Abuse. (2000). *Principles of Drug Addiction Treatment: A Research-Based Guide*. Bethesda, MD: National Institute on Drug Abuse, National Institutes of Health.

Nejtek, VA, Kaiser, KA, Zhang, B, Djokovic, M. (2013). Iowa Gambling Task scores predict future drug use in bipolar outpatients with stimulant dependence. *Psychiatry Research* 210, 871–879.

Neri, S., Signorelli, S. S., Torrisi, B., Pulvirenti, D., Mauceri, B., Abate, G., et al. (2005). Effects of antioxidant supplementation on postprandial oxidative stress and endothelial dysfunction: A single-blind, 15-day clinical trial in patients with untreated type 2 diabetes, subjects with impaired glucose tolerance, and healthy controls. Philadelphia, PA: *Clinical Therapeutics* 27(11), 1764–1773.

Neugarten, B. L., and Datan, N. (1973). Sociological perspectives on the life cycle. Thousand Oaks, CA: *The Meaning of Age*, 96–113.

Newberg, A., and d'Aquili, E. G. (2008). *Why God Won't Go Away: Brain Science and the Biology of Belief*. New York, NY: Random House LLC.

Niaura, R. (2000). Cognitive social learning and related perspectives on drug craving. London: *Addiction* 95(8s2), 155–163.

NINDS. (2002). National Institute of Neurological Disorders and Stroke Post-Stroke Fact Sheet. Bethesda, MD: *The National Institutes of Health National Institute of Neurological Disorders and Stroke, NIH Publication No. 02–4846*.

O'Brien, C. P. (2009). Neuroplasticity in addictive disorders. *Dialogues in Clinical Neuroscience* 11(3), 350.

Olds, J., and Milner, P. (1954). Positive reinforcement produced by electrical stimulation of septal area and other regions of rat brain. *Journal of Comparative and Physiological Psychology* 47(6), 419.

Onozuka, M., Fujita, M., Watanabe, K., Hirano, Y., Niwa, M., Nishiyama, K., and Saito, S. (2002). Mapping brain region activity during chewing: A functional magnetic resonance imaging study. *Journal of Dental Research* 81(11), 743–746.

Paul, L. K., Brown, W. S., Adolphs, R., Tyszka, J. M., Richards, L. J., Mukherjee, P., and Sherr, E. H. (2007). Agenesis of the corpus callosum: Genetic, developmental and functional aspects of connectivity. *Nature Reviews Neuroscience* 8(4), 287–299.

Penfield, W., and Jasper, H. (1954). *Epilepsy and the Functional Anatomy of the Human Brain*. Boston: Little, Brown.

Plotkin, W. B.; and Rice, K. M. (1981). Biofeedback as a placebo: Anxiety reduction facilitated by training in either suppression or enhancement of alpha brainwaves. *Journal of Consulting and Clinical Psychology* Vol 49(4), Aug 1981, 590–596.

Ploughman, M. (2008). Exercise is brain food: the effects of physical activity on cognitive function. *Developmental Neurorehabilitation* 11(3), 236–240.

Prescription Drug Abuse: Strategies to Stop the Epidemic. (n.d.).—Trust for America's Health. Retrieved July 29, 2014, from http://healthyamericans.org/reports/drugabuse2013/.

Ramel, W., Goldin, P. R., Carmona, P. E., and McQuaid, J. R. (2004). The effects of mindfulness meditation on cognitive processes and affect in patients with past depression. *Cognitive Therapy and Research* 28(4), 433–455.

Retz, W., Retz-Junginger, P., Schneider, M., Scherk, H., Hengesch, G., and Rosler, M. (2007). [Drug addiction in young prison inmates with and without attention deficit hyperactivity disorder (ADHD)]. *Fortschr Neurol Psychiatr* 75(5), 285–292.

Ring, K. (1982). *Life at Death: A Scientific Investigation of the Near-Death Experience*. New York: Quill.

Rubin, S. E., and Lawlis, G. F. (1970). A model for differential treatment for alcoholics. New York: *Rehabilitation Research and Practice Journal*.

Schulz, Mona (2005) *The New Feminine Brain*. New York: Free Press.

Schwartz, J.and Begley, S. (2002) *The Mind and The Brain*. New York: Harper-Collins.

Scott, W. C., Kaiser, D., Othmer, S., and Sideroff, S. I. (2005). Effects of an EEG biofeedback protocol on a mixed substance abusing population. *American Journal of Drug and Alcohol Abuse* 31(3), 455–469.

Sheikh, A. A., and Korn, E. R. (Eds.). (1994). *Imagery in Sports and Physical Performance*. Amityville, NY: Baywood Publishing Company, Inc..

Sherman, C. (2007). The defining features of drug intoxication and addiction can be traced to disruptions in cell-to-cell signaling. *NIDA Notes: National Institutes of Health, National Institute of Drug Abuse* 21(4).

Shire US Inc. (2006). *Ensuring Appropriate Stimulant Use for ADHD: A Parent's Guide to Being AWARE* [Electronic Version], 5. Retrieved January 16, 2008 from http://www.adderallxr.com/about_adderallxr/about-sideeffects.asp.

Sigafus, P. B. (2013). Can heart rate variability biofeedback increase sensory motor rhythms? (Doctoral dissertation, Alliant International University).

Skeide, S. M. (2010). *Meditation and neuroplasticity*.

Smith, E. W. L. (January 2000). *The Body in Psychotherapy*. Jefferson, NC: McFarland. p.16. ISBN 978-0-7864-8181-1.

Srinivasan, N. S. (2012). Enhancing neuroplasticity to improve peak performance. *Biofeedback* 40(1), 30–33.

Stafstrom, C. E., and Rho, J. M. (2012). The ketogenic diet as a treatment paradigm for diverse neurological disorders. *Frontiers in Pharmacology* 3.

Staud, R., Vierck, C. J., Cannon, R. L., Mauderli, A. P., and Price, D. D. (2001). Abnormal sensitization and temporal summation of second pain (wind-up) in patients with fibromyalgia syndrome. *Pain*, 91(1), 165–175.

Steinberg, L. (2004). Risk taking in adolescence: What changes, and why? New York, NY: *Annals of the New York Academy of Sciences* 1021(1), 51–58.

Suinn, R. M. (1984). Imagery and sports. *Cognitive Sport Psychology* 253–257.

Sutarto, A. P., Wahab, M. N. A., and Zin, N. M. (2010). Heart Rate Variability (HRV) biofeedback: A new training approach for operator's performance enhancement. *Journal of Industrial Engineering and Management* 3(1), 176–198.

Tarazi, F., and Schetz, J. (2005). *Neurological and Psychiatric Disorders.* Clifton, NJ: Humana Press.

Teegarden, S. L., Scott, A. N., and Bale, T. L. (May 2009). Early life exposure to a high fat diet promotes long-term changes in dietary preferences and central reward signaling. *Neuroscience* 162 (4): 924–32. doi:10.1016/j.neuroscience.2009.05.029. PMC 2723193. PMID 19465087.

Terman, M., and Terman, J. S. (2005). Light therapy for seasonal and nonseasonal depression: Efficacy, protocol, safety and side effects. *CNS Spectrums* 10(8), 647.

Thompson, A. L., Molina, B. S., Pelham, W., Jr., and Gnagy, E. M. (2007). Risky driving in adolescents and young adults with childhood ADHD. *Journal of Pediatric Psychology* 32(7), 745–759.

Tikkanen, R., Holi, M., Lindberg, N., and Virkkunen, M. (2007). Tridimensional Personality Questionnaire data on alcoholic violent offenders: specific connections to severe impulsive cluster B personality disorders and violent criminality. *BMC Psychiatry, 7*, 36.

Tinius, T. P., and Tinius, K. A. (2000). Changes after EEG biofeedback and cognitive retraining in adults with mild traumatic brain injury and attention deficit hyperactivity disorder. *Journal of Neurotherapy* 4(2), 27–44.

Uauy, R., and Dangour, A. D. (2006). Nutrition in brain development and aging: Role of essential fatty acids. *Nutrition Reviews* 64(s2), S24–S33.

Valnet, J. (2012). *The Practice of Aromatherapy.* New York, NY: Random House.

Van Stegeren, A. H., Wolf, O. T., Everaerd, W., and Rombouts, S. A. (2008). Interaction of endogenous cortisol and noradrenaline in the human amygdala. *Progress in Brain Research* 167, 263–268.

Vaschillo, E., Lehrer, P., Rishe, N., and Konstantinov, M. (2002). Heart rate variability biofeedback as a method for assessing baroreflex function: A preliminary study of resonance in the cardiovascular system. *Applied Psychophysiology and Biofeedback* 27(1), 1–27.

Vestergaard-Poulsen, P., van Beek, M., Skewes, J., Bjarkam, C. R., Stubberup, M., Bertelsen, J., and Roepstorff, A. (2009). Long-term meditation is associated with increased gray matter density in the brain stem. *Neuroreport* 20(2), 170–174.

Vlahov D., Galea S., Resnick H., et al. (June 2002). Increased use of cigarettes, alcohol, and marijuana among Manhattan, New York, residents after the September 11th terrorist attacks. *American Journal of Epidemiology* 155 (11): 988–96. PMID 12034577.

Vlodavsky, E., Palzur, E., and Soustiel, J. F. (2006). Hyperbaric oxygen therapy reduces neuroinflammation and expression of matrix metalloproteinase-9 in the rat model of traumatic brain injury. *Neuropathology and Applied Neurobiology* 32(1), 40–50.

Volkow, N. D. (2009). *Science of Addiction: Drugs, Brains, and Behavior* (rev.). Darby, PA: Diane Publishing.

White, W. (2009). *Peer-based Addiction Recovery Support: History, Theory, Practice, and Scientific Evaluation.* Chicago, IL: Great Lakes Addiction Technology Transfer Center and Philadelphia Department of Behavioral Health and Mental Retardation Services.

———. (2008). *Recovery Management and Recovery-Oriented Systems of Care: Scientific Rationale and Promising Practices.* Pittsburgh, PA: Northeast Addiction Technology Transfer Center, Great Lakes Addiction Technology Transfer Center, Philadelphia Department of Behavioral Health and Mental Retardation Services.

Whitman, R. (2012) *Intervention: A Process—Not an Event,* unpublished manuscript.

Wildmann, J., Kruger, A., Schmole, M., Niemann, J., and Matthaei, H. (1986). Increase of circulating beta-endorphin-like immunoreactivity correlates with the change in feeling of pleasantness after running. *Life Sci, 38*(11), 997–1003.

Wilson, B. (2013). Alcoholics Anonymous. Alcoholics Anonymous ("Big Book," 4th ed.) (2001). New York: AA World Services, Inc.

World Health Organization. (2004). *International Statistical Classification of Diseases and Related Health Problems* (Vol. 1). Switzerland: World Health Organization.

Wu, A., Ying, Z., and Gomez-Pinilla, F. Dietary omega-3 fatty acids normalize BDNF levels, reduce oxidative damage, and counteract learning disability after traumatic brain injury in rats. *Journal of Neurotrauma* 21.10 (2004): 1457–1467.

Index

About the Authors

Dr. Frank Lawlis received his PhD from Texas Tech University with an emphasis on rehabilitation counseling psychology and psychometrics after receiving his masters in counseling psychology and an MS in education and mathematics from the University of North Texas. He has pioneered research and clinical methods in research methodology and statistics, imagery techniques (cancer), pain perception and rehabilitation, biofeedback, transpersonal psychology, and most recently, psychoneuroplasticity. He has published twelve best-selling books incorporating these concepts and published over one hundred articles in research journals. Some of his classic books include *The ADD Answer, The IQ Answer,* and *Transpersonal Medicine.* He has served on the teaching staff of five major medical schools and has had professorships in five major medical schools, including Universities of Texas Health Science Center at Dallas and San Antonio, Texas Tech University Medical School, and Stanford Medical School. He has earned board certification in both clinical and counseling psychology from the American Board of Professional Psychology, Inc., and has been awarded the ranking of Fellow by the APA for his scientific contributions to psychology. He also has served as chief of oversite production and resource supervisor, besides being a consistent professional consultant on *The Dr. Phil Show* for twelve years.

Laura Martinez serves as the psychoneuroplasticy coordinator for Origins Behavioral Health Care in South Padre Island, Texas. She has assisted in developing novel brain plasticity interventions at Origins. Martinez received her bachelor of science degree in psychology with a minor in neuroscience and pre-medicine from Texas A&M University. She graduated with high honors from the psychology department and spent four years examining the effects of chemical dependency in the Behavioral and Cellular Neuroscience research labs of Texas A&M University, specifically studying the effects of whether perinatal lead exposure changes cocaine sensitivity long after lead exposure. She went on to attain her internship license in chemical dependency counseling. Martinez has a passion for providing supportive guidance to individuals who are battling addiction and for teaching patients the benefits and freedom brain plasticity interventions bring.